Ruff's Little Book of
BIG FORTUNES IN
GOLD & SILVER

Ruff's Little Book of
BIG FORTUNES IN
GOLD & SILVER
A Middle Class
License to Print Money

HOWARD RUFF

10 Finger Press
Soquel, CA

12/08 LAD 7/08 5(0)
4-10 LAD 2-10 7(1)

Ruff's Little Book of Big Fortunes in Gold and
Silver: A Middle Class License to Print Money

For more financial advice from Howard Ruff, go to
http://www.rufftimes.com.

ISBN 978-1-933174-96-9
LCCN 2006906546

09 08 07 06   5 4 3 2

Interior design and layout:
Ghislain Viau Creative Publishing (viaugh@colba.net)

TABLE OF CONTENTS

INTRODUCTION

T his book is deliberately designed not to be a weighty academic tome, but a small, inexpensive guide to help anyone get rich fast! Written primarily for the new, middle-class gold and silver investor in the new bull market, it is also a good quick review and serious update for the experienced gold bug. I've simplified the issues so that you can learn what I've learned the expensive, hard way about investing in gold and silver—the myths, the truths, and the whys and hows of the market.

What Idiot Would Buy Gold Just Because a Formerly Bankrupt Opera Singer Said to Do It?

More than 600,000 very smart "idiots" who believed me enough to subscribe to my award-winning newsletter, *The Ruff Times*, and almost three million buyers of my record-breaking 1977 book, *How to Prosper During the Coming Bad Years*. This bestselling book contained, among other things, a manual on why, how, and when to buy gold and silver, and made my readers as much as five to 17 times their money in the great gold and silver bull market of the '70s and early '80s.

They're about to do it again in the next few years. And you can, too.

Once I got it through my thick skull that the bull market was really over, I didn't recommend gold or silver in *The Ruff Times* for the many years they turned out to be lousy investments, so we made a lot of money in bonds and stocks. But now the silver and gold bull (really calf) markets are finally back after two decades. The worst financial decision you can make is to ignore them. This one mistake will cost you more than all the dumb financial decisions you can make put together, short of playing the roulette table in Vegas. Gold and silver are early in a historic bull market that will dwarf the 500-1,700 percent profits that millions of savvy, ignore-the-crowd middle-class investors made in the '70s.

Is this just hype? Is it unreasonable to expect such great returns? Well, in Chapter 3 I've given you a few facts to chew on, explaining why gold will hit at least $2,172. And in Chapter 5 you will learn why $100 silver is inevitable. The forces that drove gold and silver into the stratosphere in the '70s are back in spades, only more so. Several times more so!

Printing Money the High-Tech Way

The most powerful, completely essential factor affecting *gold* is *monetary inflation*–the number of dollars created out of thin air to solve society's problems and meet its demands, diluting the value of each dollar. Monetary inflation is now so great that no one knows how many dollars there are floating around in the world. In fact, the Federal Reserve, whose duty it is to create and regulate dollars, doesn't know, or doesn't want *you* to know, how many there are in existence. The Fed recently stopped reporting "M-3" every month. M-3 used to be the most widely-followed measurement of dollar growth and monetary inflation.

The most compelling force affecting *silver* today is the supply/demand equation. Soon there could be very little silver available to investors at anywhere near today's price. Uncle Sam's cupboard is bare. The government stockpiles are all gone! The centuries-long supply overhang is shrinking fast. Why? Because industrial usage is soaring, and production of new silver has plummeted during the 22-year silver and gold bear market.

There are now thousands of irreplaceable uses for silver that affect modern life, and that in part is what consumed the once-massive stockpiles. Some authorities believe there are more industrial uses for silver than any other product taken from the ground except petroleum. Also, a problem exists within the silver futures positions at the COMEX (the New York Commodity Exchange, by far the biggest commodity exchange in the world). The shorts (those who are betting against the metal by selling futures contracts) will often have to cover by silver purchases that total more than the world's production of newly mined silver.

Added to this is the fact that in the 1970's bull market, even when it was universally believed that silver supplies above ground were massive indeed, silver outperformed gold by two to one, so the stage is now set. Actually it could do much better this time as the gap between silver and gold supplies has narrowed over the years.

All these factors, including the inexorable law of supply and demand (including demand for silver by industry, jewelry fabricators, and investment—more about this in Chapter 5), are a lead-pipe-cinch guarantee of future price inflation. I don't have to speculate about the future; the future is here! It just hasn't yet been recognized by the investment community. This book is probably the first robin of spring.

If you don't have the message about gold and silver yet, you are in good company. If you watch the TV financial shows, you would think that gold and silver didn't even exist. When the issue under discussion is the falling dollar, none of the Wall Street gurus even mention gold, even though the record is clear—when the dollar is in a long-term down trend, gold soars—every time! But when inflation is the subject, Wall Street ignores the classic inflation hedges—gold and silver and mining stocks. You *never* hear from the Wall Street gurus about silver, although when gold is soaring, silver always does at least twice as well. Gold has risen from $252 to over $650 as this is written, and silver, as if it had written the script, has risen from under $4 to over $11.

And the ultimate irony is that gold and silver are so easy for unsophisticated Americans to buy:

- Coin shops that will sell you gold and silver bullion coins are as ubiquitous as fleas on a coyote. There is one within five miles of most American homes.
- If you want to put the metals in an IRA or other tax-deferred account, you can buy gold in the ground—shares of mining companies or gold mutual funds. There are lots of fine, publicly-traded mining companies and mutual funds and new gold and silver ETFs (Exchange-traded Funds) from which to choose.
- Or you can buy American gold or silver eagle coins, which are exempt from the no-bullion IRA rules.
- And you don't even have to be very smart to buy gold and silver mining stocks. When gold is in a bull market, even the

turkeys fly. You can put a list of the mining companies (see Chapter 11) on the wall, throw darts at it, invest in the holes and make money. A rising tide raises all boats.

Of course, mining companies are businesses just like other businesses, and you can really improve your performance in your favor when you know a few simple fundamentals that separate a great new mine from a hole in the ground surrounded by liars.

It's a lot like being in a time warp and going back to the '70s when the same attitudes prevailed. Back then, Wall Street acted as though the metals didn't even exist until they had risen so high ($650 gold, $30 silver) that there wasn't much profit left in them. Then they jumped in as Wall Street brokers and advisors did their usual thing–they bought high and eventually sold low.

This is cherry-picking time for contrarians, although skepticism will lead most readers to miss out on the good buys at the beginning when things are really cheap–like now. Why? No guts. That's what this book is all about–finding the guts to pick cherries when they are still cheap, just as I did in the mid '70s.

Unfortunately, I didn't get out right at the top of the bull market in the early '80s. Re-reading the Ruff Times from the '80s has been very instructive. I found it difficult back then to let go of gold when the bull market was over in 1980. I was so seduced by gold that I truly felt it would go down to $400 (good call) then bounce back to $1,000 or more (bad call). But history is a great teacher, and I'm an avid student and 25 years smarter than I was then. I'll know when it's over this time (see Chapter 15, page 89).

Gold and silver have finally been reborn, and they're still cheap. The fundamentals that drove them are back in spades, only bigger than the fundamentals that drove gold and silver in the '70s. This Golden Calf will grow up into a far bigger bull than we saw last time!

Fortunes are made by those who see the great turning points of history and bet on them early. This is one of those rare times. And often those turning points are scary enough to drive mainstream Wall Streeters to cower and sit on their money. That's one reason why the big stock market indices often go nowhere when gold and silver are rising.

This time, gold and silver (especially the mining stocks) will be a license to print money.

In this book, I'll answer six key questions:

- Why should you bet on gold and silver now?
- How far could they go before the world turns sane again?
- When should you be a gold bug, and even more important, when should you *not?*
- What kind of metals should you buy? Coins? Bullion? Gold and silver mining stocks?
- Where should you buy them?
- When should you sell them?

And while I'm on the subject of profit, I have another thing I want to get off my chest early in the game.

Warning: Money and Things of the Spirit

It is ironic to me that although I write about money, it does not run my life. For spiritual reasons, I try to live my personal life as though money is not really very important. It is too easy to get so obsessed with profits that the quest for them can consume me—if I let it happen. How you deal with money and the pursuit of it is, of course, up to you and really none of my business. But I don't want to be complicit in turning you into an acolyte of Mammon, the malevolent false god of greed, so let me briefly pause to discharge my responsibility in this matter. From there, how you handle the acquisition of wealth is up to you.

This book is about how to take advantage of the greatest, wealth-producing bull market in your lifetime. We're talking about real wealth here! Whenever I write about how to get rich on investments, I am always nervous that I will be feeding one of the seven deadly sins—greed—which is the pursuit of money for the poorest of reasons. Greed is a personal destroyer if you lose sight of more important values. You can lose your family and your spirituality. You have to keep money in perspective and in its proper rank among the things that are—or should be—important to you, and you can.

My hierarchy of things that really matter to me: 1) wife and family, 2) God and church (I'm a practicing Mormon, and I'm going to keep practicing until I get it right. But don't worry, this is not a pulpit.), 3) country, 4) charity, and in distant last place, 5) money. To me, far more important than how much money I have is what kind of person I am. Have I let money corrupt me? Am I still generous when I can truly help someone? Am I still kind and freely giving? Do I still tithe (to my church, a charity, a poor family beset by problems not of their own making, a good cause)? Do I really need that bigger house, that luxurious new car, that new boat? Do I always keep money in its proper place in my life by consistently giving some of it away? Are my wife and my posterity still the core of my life? Am I a soft touch when someone has a real need?

If you follow the advice in this book and make a fortune, will it bless your life or corrupt your soul? That's up to you.

I suggest you constantly monitor your soul. My daughter said it best: "Dad, there is only one good reason to be rich. It's so you can give it away." At first, I thought to myself, "That's easy enough for you to say. You've never been rich." Then I had a second thought; I remembered the story of the wealthy man who had led a good Christian life, but he really loved his money. Because of his righteous track record, when he died, the Lord made an exception in his case and said, "You *can* take it with you." So the man loaded up his wheelbarrow with gold and entered Heaven. As he walked through the pearly gates, two nearby angels saw him, and one said to the other, "Why is he bringing paving stones?"

'Nuff said. Now that I have this off my chest, let's get back to business and go for it!

When you've read the compelling story of gold, silver and mining stocks, you will learn how to be a winner when the Wall Street gurus are all crying in their imported beer. (More details and market updates are given every three weeks in each issue of *The Ruff Times*.)

Enjoy and profit.

CHAPTER 1

DÉJÀ VU ALL OVER AGAIN–
AND THEN SOME! WHY GOLD
AND SILVER RIGHT NOW?

"Gold has worked since Alexander's time...
When something holds good for two thousand years,
I do not believe it can be so because of prejudice
or mistaken theory."

Bernard Baruch

There are many dumb things you can do with your money in 2006, but *not buying gold or silver will cost you more money than all of them put together.* Reasons why this is so abound, but a few of them stand out, like these:

- *Gold and silver* are early in an historic bull market—in fact, as this is written; it's only a Golden Calf—making this a low-risk investment with an awesome upside!

- *This bull market will dwarf the last great one* in 1975-80 when fortunes were made by relatively small amounts of money invested by amateur investors.

- *All of the factors that created the last bull market are here again,* only several times greater, not the least of which is far more ongoing Fed money creation than in the '70s.

- *Supply figures* are inexorably racing toward even greater aboveground silver supply shortages than today, and they have already reached beyond-believable proportions. Some experts believe there is now more gold bullion than silver bullion above ground for the first time in recorded history. Rising gold and silver jewelry demand by the hundreds of millions of brand new middle class people in India and China are now an indigestible fact of life. Silver, the real monetary metal, is now also a critical industrial metal with thousands of irreplaceable applications. Meanwhile, the needs of industry can no longer be met solely from new production. Demands by investors, industry and jewelry fabricators are soaring. The investment community has not yet awakened to the stark supply/demand facts, which has created an incredible, once-in-a-lifetime opportunity.

And, *you can get there before the alleged insiders, users and experts!*

Here is the bottom line: supply and production are shrinking and demand is soaring.

These are just a few of the reasons why *ignoring* gold or silver will cost you a fortune! Gold is headed towards at least *$2,500* an ounce (currently near $560, up from $252 so far), and silver is headed for at least *$100* (currently more than $10, up from $4). And, the best by far is still ahead! You will regret ignoring this epic opportunity for the rest of your life!

Are those forecasts reasonable? Here's food for thought.

- In 1980, the historic '70s gold bull market finally topped out at $850. After adjusting for inflation, to merely equal what it did in 1981, gold would have to go only to *$2172!*

- Silver topped out at $50 in 1980. After adjusting for inflation since then, to merely equal what it did in 1981, silver would have to go to *$125!*

Then why do I believe the metals could even go much higher than that? Lots of reasons, such as the tendency of bull and bear markets to go to excessive extremes. But the most compelling is that the biggest single factor that drives gold and silver is monetary inflation, and that's several times greater now than during the great gold and silver bull market of the '70s. (More about monetary inflation in a moment.) And the silver supply/demand phenomenon means far higher prices, unless they have repealed the law of supply and demand when I wasn't looking.

CHAPTER 1

Born-Again Gold Bug

After more than 20 years of recommending against investing in gold and silver (which turned out to be darn good advice), I'm again all-out bullish on the metals, for very good, deeply-considered reasons. After nearly a quarter-century since the last spectacular bull market in gold and silver, it's "déjà vu all over again," as that noted Yankee philosopher, Yogi Berra, reminded us.

*Let me introduce–or reintroduce–myself before I go on. I've written the financial newsletter, *The Ruff Times,* for 31 years. It is not written for Wall Street, but for Main Street! When I began publishing it in July, 1975, I begged my subscribers to buy *$120* gold and *$2* silver. Five years later in 1980, I finally put out a sell recommendation. Gold was *$750* (up 500 percent), and silver was *$35,* (up 1500 percent!). They topped out two weeks later at $850 and $50 respectively, so I didn't sell at the exact top, but "close" is plenty good enough. Then for more than 20 years, I made money for my subscribers in stocks, bonds, real estate, and other traditional investments.

Partly because of my ongoing counsel during those golden years as to *what kind* of gold to buy, *why* to buy gold and silver, *where* to safely buy them–and especially–*when to sell them, The Ruff Times* became by far the biggest financial newsletter in the known universe with over 600,000 subscribers over the years. At the risk of sounding immodest (I once thought I was getting humble. It felt terrible, but I was only coming down with the flu), I probably learned at least as much about gold and silver and their markets in that bull run back then as any financial writer alive today.

But that's only part of the story. Early in 1978, my mega-bestseller, *How To Prosper During The Coming Bad Years,* sold almost three million copies, making it the biggest-selling financial book in history (and it still is). That book contained basic reasons why you should buy gold and silver, and helped to guide millions of Americans through one of the most profitable investment markets in history! It also may have been one of the factors that drove that historic bull market.

In 1980, after I finally announced in *The Ruff Times* that the bull market was over and we liquidated, I ignored the metals for 22 years–and, as it turned out, that was a very good idea. Then, in late 1999, I begged millions of Americans to sell all their stocks, shortly before the spectacular dot com bubble topped out the next April. That bubble is still dot gone after six years.

Now I've been back again in familiar territory, riding the Golden Calf since December, 2003. As the calf becomes a massive bull over the next few years, you can make a ton of money in gold, more than twice as much in silver, and a lot more than that in carefully selected mining stocks.

Maybe you missed the boat in the late '90s and didn't get in on the dot com market. You may feel you missed the chance of a lifetime. There is a new bus along every few years, a new bull market made just for you. Well, this is it!

Maybe you *did* catch the stock-market boat just before it sank, and then rode out the losses, losing money every day for months and years. Perhaps you feel so traumatized by that experience that you have decided not to take any more investment risks. There is an old saying: "a cat who sits on a hot stove won't sit on one again, but he probably won't sit on a cold stove either."

The stove is warming, but it's not yet too hot to get on again. So, let's discuss a few of the more-detailed reasons gold and silver are again safe investments with unlimited potential:

Why Gold and Silver Now?

Real money. Gold and silver (especially silver) have been real money over and over again, in all ages and on all continents. Ever since Gutenberg invented the moveable-type printing press 500-plus years ago, the world has been littered with dead-paper currencies every 50 to 75 years, due to excess money printing. Each time, gold and silver first became hugely profitable investments, then when the currency finally caved in to inflation, gold and silver or a gold-backed currency became the coin of the realm. This was the inevitable result of printing more and more pieces of paper with ink on them, no longer backed by gold or silver. Ultimately, the public caught on to the scam and refused to accept the counterfeit money in return for their hard-produced goods and services (price inflation?). And, it has happened over and over again throughout history, proving that he who refuses to remember the past is forever condemned to repeat it. Before the inevitably tragic outcomes, monetary inflation has always driven gold and silver to "unreasonable" heights.

A History of Money–the "Reader's Digest" Version

History tells us that the first paper currencies were notes payable (redeemable) in gold or silver, or, mere warehouse receipts. Over the years, it became obvious that it was easier to simply exchange the receipts after a transaction than go to the warehouse with the receipts to get the gold and silver. Paper became currency in common usage, and the people began to think of the receipts (currency) as money all by itself.

Then, as governments began to buy votes or finance wars, they yielded to the temptation to simply print more "receipts" than there was gold and silver to back them up (who would know?), each time triggering more and more inflation. The foundation for inflationary tactics was laid in America when Roosevelt created the New Deal, then Lyndon Johnson financed the War on Poverty and the Vietnam War at the same time (guns and butter), and the printing presses have had to step up the pace ever since. (Poverty won and so did North Vietnam, but that's another story.)

The process of currency destruction has been accelerating, with advances punctuated by retreats, since the '30s. Throughout history, this has been the case over and over again ever since the birth of paper money. The critical moment in this era came when Nixon "closed the gold window" (no longer allowing dollars to be exchanged for gold or silver) at the Federal Reserve. This move finally admitted America's irresponsible reality and permanently detached the paper dollars from gold, and the money printers were off to the races. (More about the *new* printing press in a later chapter.)

Then Uncle Sam hammered the last nail into the coffin in 1965 by no longer making 90 percent silver coins.

In the last ten years, the Fed has manufactured trillions of dollars out of nothing at the fastest pace in history by far, and it's accelerating. The Fed has then loaned the dollars into circulation, or given them to politicians to spend. Since then, Congress has been spending like a drunken sailor.

(The difference between Congress and a drunken sailor? A drunken sailor spends his own money!) This money expansion now dwarfs the monetary explosion which led to that historic metals bull market in the '70s. Gold and silver have been rising recently in response, driving gold from $252 to $560, and silver from $4 to more than $10.

It's hard for me to exaggerate or overstate what is happening. Economists call this monetary-expansion process "inflation." It really should be called "dilution," that is, dilution of the money supply, and consequently its value. Inevitably, this sooner or later causes rising consumer prices, which laymen, and the media, and even Wall Street, will still mistakenly call "inflation." Calling rising prices "inflation" is like calling falling trees "hurricanes!"

(Or as Jim Dines says, "it's like calling wet sidewalks rain.)

When will the masses catch on to this steadily progressing fact of life? Gold and silver prices are the true measure of public awareness. Sooner or later, awareness reaches critical mass, and the metals go through the stratosphere.

The falling dollar. One early-warning harbinger of inflation is the dollar losing exchange value against foreign currencies. The dollar, with fits and starts, has been in a long-term bear market for a few years. A falling dollar is inflationary, as it takes more and more dollars to buy the increasing amounts of foreign-produced goods we are now buying. Wal-Mart's soaring sales are a telling indicator, as they are Asia's biggest customer. Gold and oil are quoted in dollars, so up they go. And now the metals are rising, not just against the dollar, but against nearly all currencies as the metals grow in strength, and virtually every country on Earth is inflating its currency.

(It's actually more accurate to say the dollar is falling in relation to gold, than to say gold is rising in relation to the dollar).

The falling dollar-exchange value explains the early strength of the metals, and there is a lot more to come, as we continue to flood the international money markets with dollars. We now don't even have to print them. This is the age of cyber-money, when less than five percent of the dollars are minted or printed, and most are only computer entries at banks. We don't even know how many dollars there are!

Falling metals production. There is a serious supply problem. 22 years of low or falling gold and silver prices gave us a drop in production and exploration of epic proportions, as miners pulled in their horns to preserve their capital. This set the scene for a great supply/demand problem. Now that prices are high enough to make gold and silver mining profitable, it will take as long as seven to ten years to develop new mining and production, and falling supply and rising demand have made higher prices inevitable for the imminent future. (More about this in Chapter 9.)

Also, remember that most of the easy shallow silver has been mined over the centuries, even with primitive methods, and the silver deposits are still being depleted. For example, during the Roman millennium, silver coins were used for currency, so the Romans, after they conquered Spain, expropriated the large Spanish silver mines so they could use the silver for their own coins. They soon depleted the shallow mines, so they began to counterfeit their own currency, mixing silver with base metals, making the coins thinner, or clipping the corners.

As the mines were further depleted, it got worse and worse until the citizens began to distrust the currency, demanding more and more of it in exchange for their goods and services, causing a great inflation. Soon, the far-flung Roman Legions refused to accept the less-and-less valuable coins for their pay, and began deserting in droves. This inflation was one of the root causes of the fall of the Roman Empire—all because they depleted the shallow silver mines.

Now, as silver industrial applications have soared (see Chapter 5), there are few satisfactory substitutes in sight. New silver mines are getting harder and more expensive to find, and supply is falling farther and farther short of demand. One expert claims that the deeper you go into the ground, the less silver there is.

Vanishing Inventory. Both metals are far rarer than most people know. All the *gold* ever mined since the dawn of history, including that in central banks, gold fillings and sunken shipwrecks in the Caribbean, would cover a football field about four feet deep. And, demand is now leaping past new supplies.

Jewelry demand. China and India are enjoying a historic burst of capitalist prosperity, and their booming new middle class is enthusiastically buying gold and silver jewelry, creating soaring new demand!

Silver use is incredible and rising! There are thousands of irreplaceable silver industrial uses, which accounts for the shrinking inventory. Government silver warehouses are now all empty, and COMEX futures positions, much of which must be covered eventually by deliveries or purchases, are estimated to be *equal to or greater than all new production!*

Silver is the poor man's gold. Think of gold as large denomination money, and silver as small change. A one-ounce gold coin now costs only about $650, and you can buy a roll of pre-1965, 90 percent-silver dimes for close to $50 a roll. Partly because it is so much cheaper that the potential buying pool is much larger, and industrial use is so much greater, *silver will be more profitable than gold by at least 100 percent!*

And, there's more to come.

CHAPTER 2

THE GOLD AND
SILVER MYSTIQUE

Gold and silver have been symbols of wealth throughout history, far more precious in our consciousness than any mere paper substitutes for them. Ever since the printing press made paper currency possible, gold and silver coins as a means of exchange and a store of value have always bounced back. In the past whenever a society lost confidence in paper decorated with ink, and it inevitably loses its usefulness as a store of value (that is, inflates), we instinctively turn back to gold and silver. And there is a reason deeply embedded in the human psyche: the True Gold and Silver Myths!

The True Gold Myths

No other reality-based myth has been as durable as the one surrounding gold. Gold is the classic example of wealth, memorialized in myth and legend by the Chinese, the Egyptians, the Mayans, the Aztecs, the Romans, the Greeks and the Jews. Spanish conquistadores and Portuguese explorers died in the pursuit of gold. When the Spanish conquered Central and South America, they sent so much gold back to Europe (when it wasn't sent instead to the bottom of the Caribbean in a shipwreck), that the new flood of gold and silver coins (the money supply) triggered a 200-year inflation in Europe. And even now, in India and the Middle East, gold and silver are often melted down into jewelry and worn for security and as a display of wealth.

Gold not only signifies wealth, but the image of it also implies being blessed or being a winner: We've all heard of The Golden Boy, the Pot of Gold at the End of the Rainbow, The Golden Touch, The Golden

Rule (he who has the gold makes the rules), the Goose That Laid the Golden Eggs, and the Gold Medal for the winner. A flashing gold tooth is a symbol of prestige in many cultures. Golden engagement and wedding rings are recognized all over the world as a symbol of life-long bonding through marriage.

The Silver Lining

Then there is silver. The "silver lining in every cloud" is the symbol of optimism. It is right up there along with gold and platinum for jewelry.

Silver has been, by far, the most commonly-used monetary metal, including such currencies as the pound sterling. Silver coins have been standard currency in many nations in all ages, even more than gold. This is due to the tendency of silver deposits to be much shallower than gold deposits, making silver easier and cheaper to mine, even by primitive methods.

Unique Characteristics

Gold is the more malleable of the two metals. It can be spun out into a thread fine enough to be nearly invisible to the naked eye. It can be pounded out into a plate so thin that light can pass through it. It won't rust, tarnish or corrode. It will look the same in 1,000 years as it does now. All the gold ever mined would make a cube the size of an eight-room house.

Gold bonds well with other metals to form alloys of varying purity, and almost all of the gold ever mined is still in existence.

Silver is by far the more important industrial metal. It is used in thousands of applications. It can be polished to be more reflective than any other metal, which is why it is used as backing for glass to make mirrors. It has thousands of essential uses in industry, which I cover in detail in Chapter 5. For example, it is an essential component in the manufacture of all audio and video tape, and all film. But above all, it is and has been routinely accepted as money, especially in India, China, Rome, Ancient America and the Middle East.

The reasons silver is now less abundant will be explained in Chapter 5, and there is no satisfactory substitute for many of the applications.

CHAPTER 3

RIGHT AND WRONG REASONS FOR INVESTING IN GOLD AND SILVER

There are serious uses for gold and silver that have little to do with investment, and "gold bugs" often get the two confused. You need to know the difference.

The metals have three basic uses:

1. Gold and silver coins as insurance (non-investment).
2. Government holdings of gold and silver backing for the currency (non-investment).
3. Gold and silver for investments when things are right, and only then.

The first two uses fit all times and all seasons, but for number 3, timing is critical.

Gold and Silver Insurance

You should always own gold and silver coins as a financial-calamity insurance policy during both bull and bear markets. This is a perennial principle–every day, every month, and every year! Like homeowner's or automobile insurance, its purpose is to protect you against the possible but unseen economic and political calamities that you hope never happen.

It's there to use as real money in the case of a worst-case inflationary currency collapse. Or if (for example) hackers were to shut down the power grid, denying everyone access to their dollars at the bank or at the ATM. Or making it impossible to open the supermarket cash registers. Or the insertion of a destructive virus into the computers of the money-center banks, causing the world's dollars in cyberspace to disappear in a nanosecond (see Chapter 7).

Remember, only about 5 percent of the worlds' dollars are minted, printed or coined. The rest only exist on bank computers. When my wife Kay and I recently got a home-equity loan, the bank just created the money out of thin air and put it into our account. We never saw a penny of it in the physical world.

If the computer data is wiped out, the world's monetary system would disappear. The dollar is the world's reserve currency. This would mean the instant collapse of the American economy, and maybe Western civilization. The world would instinctively go back to gold and silver as a means of exchange and store of value until the computers were fixed and a new gold-backed paper-monetary system was cobbled together.

These things seem to be unthinkable in our otherwise comfortable world. But we have never had such an enemy as the murderous Islamo-fascists devoted to America's destruction, with no regard for their personal comfort, well-being, or even their lives. Not even their petro-dollars! (More about this in Chapter 7.)

Insurance Action Steps

In the event of the possible dire world outcomes I have speculated on, gold and silver will explode in value.

Each family should have at least one half-bag of pre-1965, commonly circulated, 90- percent silver dimes, quarters and half-dollars, amounting to 715 ounces of silver. This is called "junk silver," and can be bought from any neighborhood coin dealer. A bag weighs about 55 pounds. The price you pay will be that day's value of the 715 ounces of silver, plus a small premium. As this is written, bags are going for a bit over $9,000, and half bags for about $4,500.

Your insurance coins may become a fantastic investment, which they may not have been when you bought them. In the case of less drastic events, such as mere rising price inflation, they will also be profitable. The coins are fast disappearing, and you had better hurry or you might have to pay an additional premium.

Because of the critical supply/demand situation outlined in Chapter 5, you, as the holder of any form of physical silver, will find that the industries in need of them will have to bid up the price until you are willing to part with yours. $100 an ounce, anyone?

This is a buying decision for all seasons, and it only becomes an investment if bad or even mildly bad things (like rising inflation) happen in the world. *This is not for short-term profit, but for long-term protection.* You would really need your coins if a monetary crisis or a war gets bad enough and lasts long enough so that we start to universally use coins as the alternative "real" currency. It might not take long for merchants to get the drift. During the OPEC gas crisis of the '70s, when inflation and silver were in a runaway mode and gas prices were exploding, a few enterprising gas-station operators were advertising gas for a dime a gallon—pre-1965, 90-percent silver dimes. At the time, a silver dime was worth more than a gallon of gas at the posted price.

Like all insurance, these coins are there to use in case of events you hope won't happen. You win your bet only if you have a car crash, or a fire, or if you die. With orthodox insurance, it doesn't matter if you win or lose your bet, the premiums are gone forever. In the case of coin insurance, the premiums are still there and appreciating, no matter what.

Gold And Silver As Monetary Backing: a Condensed History

In theory, America should be backing its currency with gold and silver, making it fully exchangeable into the metals, as had been done for almost two centuries. That's a principled cause that dedicated gold bugs should fight for! While this is very important, it has nothing to do with investing in gold or silver.

Let me reiterate the paper money issue stated earlier: Paper money was originally invented as merely a warehouse receipt for gold or silver (real money). When holders of the receipts found it much easier to merely accept and pass on the receipts when they made transactions (rather than go to the warehouse to get the metal), the receipts became "as good as money," and then money itself. The receipts had evolved into gold- and silver-backed currency.

Still not too bad, but as we began to vote ourselves benefits from the public treasury, government started to print and issue more receipts than there was gold or silver in the warehouses—which we now called "banks." Who would know, as long as not too many receipt-holders showed up at the bank to exchange them for gold or silver?

For a long time we had confidence in the "gold and silver backing." But human nature never changes. Soon we got so accustomed to our government benefits, paid in receipts, that we accepted the printing of more and more receipts. In fact, we were oblivious to the monetary inflation. The only signs were price inflation and rising gold and silver.

The stage was finally set when it became obvious to foreign dollar-holders that there was not enough metal to meet all demands, so they began jostling to be the first in line to redeem dollars at "the Gold Window." Nixon finally faced the reality that there soon would be more receipts presented for redemption than there was gold or silver available. Until then, foreign governments were still able to exchange their dollars for the metals. But Nixon could see that we were steadily running out of gold, as foreign confidence in the paper dollar sagged so badly due to monetary inflation that we were soon threatened with losing all our gold reserves.

So Nixon closed the "gold window" at the Federal Reserve to stem the tide, and the process was complete. The dollar was now completely detached from gold and silver, and greenbacks were now just a "fiat currency." That is, real money just because a government order, or "fiat," declared it such.

Once we were comfortable (or ignorant) that the horse was out of the barn, there was no longer any worry about whether or not we had enough gold and silver in the bank to redeem the ever-growing supply of banknotes. The claims on government "entitlements" were soaring, so inflation was the inevitable consequence of money creation. Along with that, Uncle Sam began an anti-gold campaign to demonetize the metal and separate it in the public mind from "money." They even began marketing gold and silver coins (eagles) as a "mere commodity." However, enough investors understood the monetary history of gold and silver that the metals rose at the slightest hint of economic growth and subsequent threat of inflation. And, since gold was an internationally-traded commodity and a lot of foreigners had not bought into the U. S. anti-gold propaganda, the price began to rise.

"You Can't Go Home Again"

Restoring gold and silver backing to the currency would seem to be the obvious solution. But it won't work until we are willing to forego our soaring government benefits and accept the discipline gold and silver backing provide. We'd all need a sudden rush of brains to the head and character to the heart—and wallet!

Don't hold your breath! If you think this will happen, I have a bridge over the East River to sell you. It won't happen until the present money system has totally collapsed and we have nothing to lose by replacing it with an honest, hard-money system. Now, we collectively feel we have too much to lose. We have a huge vested interest in the status quo—our welfare, our Social Security, our farm subsidies, etcetera.

As a matter of principle, we of course should be in favor of gold backing for money. And this has no relation to whether or not you should invest in gold or silver.

Investing In Gold and Silver

Now let's get to the fun stuff—making money with gold and silver.

This is a matter of timing, and now is the time. You should only invest when enough of the essential factors are lined up, as they are right now. When not enough of the essential elements are there, gold and silver are lousy investments, as they were for 22 years. Now that all the factors *are* lined up, they will remain that way for years. In all probability, during the first few years of this golden bull market, you will eventually make money in the metals, no matter when you bought them or how much you paid for them. Any investment in gold and silver at almost any price will eventually pay off, Although the long-term prospects are terrific, the metals can be near-dead for years at a time—like those nearly two decades between the end of the last bull market in 1980 and the beginning of the current one.

After I finally gave up on the metals in the 1980s, I watched gold and silver go sideways and down for many years. As it was not the right time for the metals, we made our money in carefully selected stocks, bonds, and real estate for more than two decades while keeping an eye out for today's conditions.

So what conditions are favorable to gold investment?

Money-creation (that is, "monetary inflation") must be in a long-term uptrend. That is the case right now, and has been for years, even during the 22-year metals bear market. So far, so bad, but alone it is not enough to cause a gold bull market.

The dollar losing exchange value against foreign currencies. This is so essential that when the dollar finally entered its current decline it finally prompted me to turn bullish as I was doing the final edits on my last book in December, 2003. Without a weakening dollar on the exchange markets, any moves in the metals will be temporary. Now we not only have that, but we have moved beyond it into the next currency phase–the metals rising against *all* currencies, which is immensely bullish.

War or the prospect of war. The war on terror and the war in Iraq are beginning to meet this condition, although the battles have been contained mostly to the Middle East. War breaking out elsewhere in the world–a terrorist nuclear, biological or bacteriological attack, or Iranian fanaticism triggering a nuclear war–would meet this requirement. We're on the brink, but not there yet. War is a wild card because it triggers inflation due to wartime spending and national and international fear. It is basically unpredictable

Not *all* of the conditions have to be met at the same time, but the first two conditions I listed are essential. War would help! Wait! Hold it a minute; that sounds perverse!

Summary

Remember, gold and silver have investment and non-investment uses, and they are not directly related. It could be argued, however, that gold and silver non-backing for the currency leads to inflation and all of its ills, and that is true. We could also argue that the insurance use of junk silver and gold coins can become an investment in a metals bull market, and that is an added benefit. But buying the metals strictly for investment purposes is a timing matter–not for short-term timing–but for timing long-term bull and bear markets.

Fortunately, the timing is right, and even if the bull is still a calf, the decision when to invest in the metals is now a moot question and will be for some years. *Just do it*, using the guidelines I will teach you in subsequent chapters.

CHAPTER 4

WHY ARE GOLD (AND SILVER) "BAD-NEWS BULLS?"

"Gold is to monetary policy what the North Star is to determining location."

Steve Forbes

Gold and silver tend to do well when everything else is going to hell. They are a pessimist's dream come true. But for realistic optimists who look for silver linings in clouds, bad news is good news indeed.

When the stock market or real estate is in the grip of inflation or an inflation-induced recession or depression like we may soon see, or stagflation like we saw in the '70s, gold and silver will thrive. The worse things get, the higher they will go. They are the classic contrarian investments.

When all commodities are in a bull market (like now), gold and silver are the only hard commodities the typical middle-class American can buy. Unlike zinc or copper or steel or soybeans, you don't have to take on a lot of risk, as with a leveraged futures contract, or have a truck back up to your door and dump a pile of copper on your porch. You can simply go to your corner coin dealer, pay cash, and walk away with gold or silver, or simply buy them in the ground–a gold or silver mining stock like any other stock.

With mining stocks and gold mutual funds, you really only have to watch one indispensable fundamental: the price of the metals. When they go up, all the mining stocks go up. When the wind blows, even the turkeys fly. Of course, some will fly much higher than others for fundamental reasons–production, property potential, management, sufficient capital, etc. *My job is to help you pick the best.*

Let me digress for a moment for a dissertation on dysfunctional and functional investor attitudes.

Pollyanna

Over the years, I have been attacked by Wall Street and the media as a gloomy pessimist, given the fact that I roared into prominence in the late '70s with my forecasts of recession, inflation, rising gold and silver, bear markets on Wall Street, emergency food storage, etc. Even though most of those things happened, Wall Street and mainstream media always bothered me because I am by nature a realistic optimist with a usually sunny disposition. I hated it when *The New York Times* did a feature on me and called me a "Prophet (sometimes spelled 'Profit') of Doom," a title that was picked up by papers all over America. Too often, journalists writing a story about me ignored the "How to Prosper" part of my book, *How to Prosper During the Coming Bad Years*, and focused only on the "Bad Years."

That was a badly distorted interpretation of optimism and pessimism that really has little to do with my thinking. Then again, I'm no Pollyanna. This famous literary character always saw the bright side of things, and ignored the dark side. Partly because of her, we have always thought of those who see the glass as half-full as "good," and those who see the glass as half-empty as "bad." But optimism and pessimism have nothing to do with reality. They are attractive or unattractive emotional states of mind and may or may not be in tune with the world as it is.

For a further example, gold and silver prosper when things happen that are considered to be "bad," especially on Wall Street. Associated with gold and silver bull markets are "bad things" such as inflation, war, and bear markets. It is natural for Wall Streeters to be optimistically bullish on the stock market. It is their baby, and the source of their income–commissions! It is also natural for them to reject bullish gold and silver forecasts, which coincide with bearish stock market forecasts. Their clients don't buy stocks when Wall Street is bearish, only when they say that the market is going up. Their views are not rooted in reality, and may be right or wrong at any given time.

For example, just one week before the top of the dot com bubble in the market in March, 2000, a survey of Wall Street advisors and market analysts produced these results: 95 percent of their recommendations said "buy," and 5 percent of them were "hold." Within a month, one of the biggest bear markets in history began.

Although the Dow Industrials have been in a two-year rally as this is written and are struggling to break above a new six-year high, NASDAQ, which is now much bigger than the Dow, has been down 55 to 60 percent for the last six years from its April 2000 high. During much of this time, Wall Street sentiment has been relentlessly bullish. Sometimes they have been right for awhile, sometimes for a year or two at a time, but only because a stopped clock is right twice a day!

That explains why Wall Street is historically down on gold and silver. Usually they're either actively against it as a holding for their clients, or acting as if it doesn't exist. They don't make any commissions on client decisions to invest in metal. They could recommend gold mining stocks or ETFs (Gold or silver exchange-traded funds; see below), or gold mutual funds, but if they do, there aren't many of them available. Those stocks are a tiny proportion of the stocks available to brokers.

If you added up the capitalization of all the mining stocks in the world, plus the value of all the gold available to the market, it would be less than the market capitalization of Microsoft or Google. A tiny bit of increased volume would bid them out of sight. If half of the brokers in the world became gold bugs, there wouldn't be anywhere close to enough merchandise to accommodate them. Their pessimism about the metals is easy to understand, as measured against their self interest. But it has *nothing* to do with reality!

Exchange-traded Funds

A case in point was reported in an article in the March 31, 2006 *Wall Street Journal*. Silver had just made a dramatic move over the two preceding days, and had hit the highest price since December, 2003. Good news, right? Wrong! *The Journal* missed the point by observing, "…it isn't a supply crunch or jewelry demand that is making silver dear." They went on to observe that all this was caused by the imminent approval of a new silver ETF–exchange-traded fund. (I will cover ETFs in detail in Chapter 5.) Now, it is true that the silver ETF will probably open up silver investing to more orthodox traders, and provide commissions to brokers, which will cause them to be more likely to recommend it. That's good, and bullish, but not a word about the metal's monetary role and value. Then *The Journal* proceeded to damn silver with faint praise. They were obviously on uncomfortable ground. I doubt if anyone was converted to silver as a result of that article. But hey, it was better than nothing–almost! I'll take anything we can get.

New let's look at a classic example of a man who saw the silver lining when surrounded by dark clouds.

A Real Pollyanna; an Optimist with Guts

Proctor & Gamble was a small seller of quality soap when the Great Depression of the early '30s hit. All of their competitors, driven by fear of loss, cut their marketing budgets and hunkered down to wait for better times. That's what most of Proctor & Gamble's scared shareholders wanted them to do. After all, financially strapped customers were defecting to cheaper brands. P&G's sales dropped 28 percent in 1933, and their stock fell more than 70 percent.

But P&G was blessed with one of the most gifted presidents in American business history, Richard Deupree. Despite the Depression, Deupree noted, some non-soap companies were prospering, and consumers were even buying luxury items like *radios*–and those consumers still needed soap.

To make a long story short, Deupree decided to ride the crest of this new wave and use it as a new advertising medium. He knew that in that day, before the invention of all of our labor-saving devices, housewives had hours of backbreaking and tedious work, with little to break the boredom–until radio.

He decided to use radio to pitch P&G's soap. After a period of trial and error, he invented the "soap opera," which captured a growing army of hard-working housewives who had to know what was happening every day to "Ma Perkins," or "Our Gal Sunday," or "Mary Noble, Backstage Wife." The characters used Oxydol and Ivory and Rinso, and listeners bought it by the carloads in preference to cheaper generic brands. Proctor & Gamble became one of the giants of American industry, and is still an icon of marketing to be studied at MBA schools.

The point is, all of P&G's cheap competitors are gone, and P&G owns the cleaning-products industry. And all because Deupree looked for the lining in the dark clouds in the worst economic depression in modern history. I have no fear of contradiction when I say that I believe Deupree probably would have seen the virtues of gold and silver in the '70s in inflationary dark clouds.

If you are a realistic optimist like me, you are always looking for the silver (or gold) linings in the gathering clouds. I just want to be right. Not because my ego requires it, but because in my profession, being wrong costs your readers money and opportunities. True optimism includes realistically looking for opportunities among bad developments. That is why gold and silver are bad-news bulls!

When I did a recent radio interview, the host, who was basically friendly, said, "You've always liked gold." My response? "No, no, no. In my investment career, I was bullish on gold for my first six years in the newsletter business, then bearish for 22 years until December, 2003. I've been bullish again for more than two years. But I guess I can never shake the label of "gold bug" which I earned way back in the 70s."

You can't be bullish about gold and silver if you think everything will be hunky dory in the world at large. The influences that drive the metals are unpleasant for the status quo. I can only be bullish on gold and silver if I believe the dollar will be sinking, inflation will be on the march, the stock market will probably decline, and scary things are happening in the world that will get worse. In that case, a true optimist must look for the aforementioned silver linings!

If the world should suddenly turn sane and the metals should tube, the true optimist will cut his potential losses and look for new opportunities, as I did for the 22 years during the gold bear market after we sold our gold and silver in 1980. Now, we are in the early years of a stock bear market. When it and the gold bull market have run their course, if the economy has hung together, we should be able to tack *The Wall street Journal* stock listings to the wall, throw darts at it, and invest in the holes the dart picks. But for now, we must invest in the silver and gold until it is stock-dart time.

Ironically, gold bugs can be just as ideologically blind as stock brokers. Many of those who were ideologically turned on to gold because of its insurance uses, or their crusade to reinstall the gold standard, confused those things with gold's merits as an investment.

Ideology is the enemy of investment, because it obscures reality. You can be a Pollyanna on either side of the gold and silver fence, and may be right or wrong, but not because of your optimism. You need to be an optimist to perceive opportunity when things don't measure up to the world you would like to see, as opposed to a realistic view of the world and the markets as they really are. A real optimist knows when and when not to bet the farm when everybody else is expecting a drought.

Although optimism and pessimism are states of mind, and have nothing to do with truth, they have a lot to do with guts–the ability to be comfortable looking north when everyone else is looking south. I may be wrong about a lot of things, but I try to be driven by realism and objective truth, not some socially-approved state of mind.

CHAPTER 5
SILVER LININGS

"**N**ever before have government silver coffers been so bare."

"Silver is used in more applications than any other commodity (aside from petroleum)."

Those are the words of Theodore Butler, an independent silver analyst. I agree with Butler that, despite the insanely profitable gold bull market, silver may not be just *twice* as profitable as gold in the next few years, but even exceed that number. Why?

Butler adds that "silver is in huge short supply, and the shortage is getting worse by the day. The silver inventories which depressed the price for more than sixty years are gone!" More about this in a moment. He's certainly right—if you are talking about silver *at today's price*!

When Jimmy Carter decided in the '70s that rising gold was an embarrassment to the dollar, he announced gold sales from Fort Knox to depress the price. But, unlike gold 35 years ago, government now can't decide to dump their silver onto the market to artificially suppress the price—because they no longer have any! Silver is still the poor man's gold, and the time is nearing when the investment world finally wakes up to the shortages. I believe that the soaring demand will make it difficult to find any investment silver at any price this side of $100 an ounce.

In the inexorable law of supply and demand, price is the great equalizer. There is plenty of silver available—at the right price—and $10 (as this is written) is not the right price. At increasingly higher prices, silver jewelry and sterling silver will come out of the woodwork. I remember back in 1980 when I put out my famous silver sell signal, Investment Rarities—which at the time was my only recommended dealer—made millions buying, melting down and salvaging all kinds of silver–sterling silver, silver jewelry and bags of coins. Investors who believed me that the silver bull market was over, were even melting down heirloom sterling silver.

The same thing will happen again, but at much higher prices. And silver will come out of India and China in the form of jewelry to be melted down, but again, at much higher prices. At these low prices, with their economic boom over the last decade, the newly created middle-class Indians and Chinese are buying gold and silver jewelry with their new wealth.

Says Butler, "If you could find a commodity which was considered a precious metal and was far more rare than gold, wouldn't today's crazy price discrepancy ($12 silver and $600 gold) seem utterly ridiculous?" I agree. But not necessarily for the same reasons as Butler. When the world discovers the supply and demand fundamentals, silver will be the star for investors. The safest money will be made in physical silver. Some day soon, the users who need it may not be able to buy physical silver at anywhere near today's price because there won't be any available in the empty warehouses. If they need or want some, they may have to buy yours or metals from India or China–at a much higher price!

Controversy

Butler is not the only sophisticated silver investor with fixed opinions on the subject. There are other very savvy gold and silver bulls who, although they challenge Butler's supply figures, believe that silver will rise spectacularly, not because of shrinking supply, but because of *rising demand.*

Let me make it clear that this controversy is not about whether or not you should invest in silver for great profits, but over the reasons *why!* It's not like Christians arguing with atheists about whether or not Christ was the divine Son of God, or if He even existed. It's more like diverse Christian believers, such as Catholics and Southern Baptists, arguing over which has the true Christian theology, while they all believe Christ was the Son of God who died for our sins.

Exchange-traded Funds

One very savvy investor, who has big mining holdings all over the word on at least three continents, believes that the new gold and silver ETFs (Exchange-traded Funds) mean a big increase in demand. I agree. The new silver ETF is called **iShares Silver Trust (AMEX: SLV)**. The rationale goes like this:

Since ETFs are a lot like mutual funds, instead of buying stocks for the ETF portfolio, the fund will have to buy gold or silver bullion as investor money pours in. Unlike mutual finds, ETFs have some advantages: you can buy or sell your shares at any hour of the day, rather than waiting until the market closes to determine your buy or sell price. They also carry the usual commission for the broker.

This opens up a huge new market for the metals. Until now, stockbrokers have been hostile to the metals for very simple reasons of self-interest. Why would they want to recommend that their clients sell some of their stocks, take the money out of the brokerage account and run off to a coin dealer and put it into bullion where there is nothing in commissions for the broker? Also, until now, main-stream investors have been unwilling to buy bullion because they know too little about it.

Now the broker can recommend shares of the gold or silver ETF, make his usual commission, and the money remains in the account. The investor is now buying silver or gold but is on familiar-feeling ground.

This will unleash a lot of buying power into a very thin market, and is immensely bullish. Demand will soar, and so will the price.

I don't know if Butler is right or not about supply, but I do know the other investors *are* right about demand, and *they both may be right!* However the controversy is resolved by time and the facts, long-term investors may make as much as ten times their money–and maybe a lot more–before it is all done. All sides of the debate agree that we will make a lot of money in silver over the long haul.

Remember, silver went from under $2 to $50 in the last bull market, when the orthodox consensus was that there was a lot more silver than gold above the ground, so the supply figures probably are not the controlling factor. With the ETFs and other factors, demand will surely soar.

One other point my savvy friend made is that silver is "a very dangerous investment" because of its volatility. He's both right and wrong. For the patient long-term investor, silver is not a dangerous investment, because it is very cheap now, and will ultimately go a lot higher. But for *the stock day trader* and *the commodities trader*, futures and short-term or day-trading the gold or silver stocks are no-nos. Why?

Deadly Futures

Let's look at futures contracts first. If you buy a futures contract for any commodity, including gold or silver, you are highly leveraged, and a comparatively small decline can wipe out your margin. Your broker will then give you perhaps the only free advice he will ever give you–a margin call! You will have to put up more money, or you will be liquidated, and there goes your margin money. That's exactly what happened a few days before I wrote this. The metals had experienced a spectacular two weeks, and we were all counting our beautiful profits. Then gold and silver had a hellacious day. For example, silver was down about *14 percent* in that one day. There was a raft of margin calls, and a lot of futures traders were wiped out. But holders of the physical metal just worried a little for a few days, if they even knew about it. Silver has since recovered and gone to new highs, then had another scary correction.

How about the mining stocks? I got a call from one of my sons who, unbeknownst to me, had bought some silver stocks based on what he thought were my recommendations. He had just gotten whacked in the general retrenchment of silver. He asked, "Dad, what do I do now?" My answer, "Son, don't ever try to trade the mining stocks. They are much too volatile, unless you are quick on your feet and spend the day in front of your computer. This is a *long-term* bull market."

So, are gold and silver dangerous? *Only* if you are thinking short-term or in leveraged volatile instruments like futures contracts. If you have physical gold or silver or fully-owned mining stocks, you just wait it out, or use the dips to buy more. Declines are great opportunities.

I will never buy gold or silver futures. Every time I've done that, I've had my head (and my empty wallet) handed to me. I don't have the temperament or the time to be continually watching the computer screen as a short-term trader. Amateur futures traders get killed over and over again, until they are broke or just give up.

Even today I will often meet someone who says, "Howard, I took your advice in the '70s and bought gold and lost a lot of money. I'll never listen to you again." Invariably, upon further questioning, he admits he bought gold or silver *futures* and got caught in a short-term correction. I don't tell anyone to buy futures for the above reasons.

So, what are the lessons here? Avoid futures contracts, unless you are a very quick-on-your-feet trader who is prepared to accept some big losses to balance against the profits to be made later. Never meet a margin call. And don't try to short-term-trade the stocks. For futures speculators and day traders, this is a very dangerous market. In the bull market of the '70s, I saw retreats of as much as 30 percent along the way to the eventual huge profits. They could wipe out futures traders in a day.

As a matter of fact, just before we went to press, the fast-moving and volatile gold and silver markets have been clobbered by a scary 30% correction.

What is the proper strategy for long-term investors in silver bullion or mining stocks? Simple. Be patient and wait out the declines, or treat these temporarily falling investments as opportunities to buy more. I actually lust after those retreats. I will be marketing my newsletter like crazy for a few years and I want to get my new subscribers into the markets as cheaply as possible.

How, Where, and When to Buy Silver

You have a lot of choices here, some better than others, and some just plain bad. Let me count the ways:

Junk Silver: Remember that the government stopped making 90 percent silver coins after 1964. These commonly circulated coins can still be bought from local coin dealers (see Appendix A for recommended dealers) by the bag or half-bag. A bag contains pre-1965 dimes, quarters and half dollars, weighs about 55 pounds, and the coins contain 715 ounces of silver. As this is written, a bag costs a bit more than

$7,000. The coin industry calls this "junk silver." These "circulated" coins have no numismatic (rare-coin) value. You will not pay their face value, but rather the current value of the silver in the bag, plus a small premium. Many of them are being scrounged out of circulation and melted down into bullion bars. By the time you read this, there may be a rising premium. Pay it. It's worth it!

Silver Bullion bars: For larger amounts of silver, you can buy Engelhard or Johnson-Matthey $100 bars and store them in a safe depository. They can be bought from any of the coin-and-bullion dealers listed in the Appendix. If they are to be stored any place other than where you bought them, or you have taken personal possession of them, they will have to be assayed when you sell them, which can be expensive and time consuming. If they are in storage, be sure they are in trust with an independent trustee. I don't really like them for the above reasons.

Silver rounds: Some private mints have manufactured some coin-like "rounds" which you can buy from a coin dealer for very little premium.

Semi-numismatic coins: These coins have some of the features of rare coins and bullion. Their price is based on both their rarity and the value of the bullion they contain. They are especially interesting for more than one reason: the numismatic value is based on their age, their condition, and the amount of bullion in them. However, the bullion content gives them a price floor, because if they ever lose their scarcity value, they can never be worth less than their bullion value. There is a lot more detail in Chapter 13 on these. I really like them a lot.

Silver in the ground: Silver mining stocks will be huge winners in the next few years. They are leveraged to the price of bullion, and will grow much faster than coins. For a lot more on this, see Chapter 11 about gold-mining and silver stocks. *They will be like a license to print money!*

ETFs: As I mentioned at the top of this chapter, a silver ETF (Exchange-traded Fund) has been recently launched and is sold on the American Exchange *(iShares Silver Trust – AMEX: SLV)*. It is a convenient way to buy silver. You can buy or sell your shares of the ETF at will, just like stocks. They will trigger a lot of silver buying, and are a very-bullish development as it exposes million of potential, non-traditional investors to the silver. The ETFs will also have to buy huge amounts of silver to meet their legal obligations, which will be a big demand factor. We'll be watching them closely to be sure they do the required buying.

What Not to Buy

Futures Contracts: My previous cautionary note about silver futures still holds! These are heavily leveraged, because you only have to put up a fraction of the value of the silver in the contract. But if silver takes a temporary nosedive, which it will, probably more than once—even as little as 10 percent—you will get a margin call from your broker, requiring you to put up more cash. As silver goes up, and if you don't get a margin call along the way, you *will* make a lot more money than if you own physical silver.

But if it temporarily goes down, you will lose your money a lot faster. If you have 10 percent margin and silver goes up, you will make ten times more money. But if silver goes down, you will lose money ten times faster. Futures are only for those with a lot of money to risk, and nerves of steel. Most of you should avoid them, and the highly-leveraged profits in mining stocks may be just as profitably leveraged, as explained in Chapter 11. The COMEX futures-contract exposure is at least greater than all the annual silver production.

This form of paper silver will boom price-wise as long as bullion does, but in the long run, by far the most safety will be found with physical silver. If independent silver analyst Theodore Butler is right and there isn't enough inventory left for silver users to get delivery settlement on their futures contracts to meet their commercial needs, they will be forced to raise their bids so they can induce you to sell them yours.

Where Did The Silver Go?

A lot of the world's underground silver deposits were laid down very shallow when God created the Earth, so it has been easily mined over the years. Most of the world's easy, cheap silver has been dug up. The world now needs increasingly hard-to-find-and-mine deposits. There is continuing production of by-product silver found along with copper and other minerals,, but most of the old, easy, pure silver mines have been depleted or are getting harder and more expensive to mine.

The world's biggest supply of above-ground silver is in India, but it's not in warehouses owned by the government. It is in the form of jewelry, worn by millions of Indians to reflect their wealth. No one person or government can decide to sell a lot of reserves for any reason. It will take mass psychology, and that will take much higher prices.

Modern Usage

Silver is a ubiquitous and essential industrial metal with literally thousands of uses, many of which are irreplaceable. This, plus sagging production, largely explains much of Butler's scenario about the disappearing inventories. *Jim Cook*, president of *Investment Rarities* (one of our recommended coin dealers, *1-800-328-1860*), recently listed just a few of silver's thousands of modern uses—many of which are counted in infinitesimal amounts per unit, but multiplied by many millions of units, it's thousands of tons of silver. I can't vouch for each one of these uses on Jim Cook's list, but most of them are true for sure; for example:

- Both rechargeable and disposable batteries are manufactured with silver alloys. Billions of silver zinc-oxide batteries are supplied to the world's market yearly, including batteries for watches, cameras and small electronic devices, tools, and TV cameras.
- Steel bearings are often electroplated with high-purity silver. Silver solder facilitates the joining of materials. Silver-brazing alloys are used in air conditioning, refrigeration, power distribution, automobiles and airplanes.
- Silver is of first importance to plumbers, appliance manufacturers, and electronics.
- Some chemical reactions use silver as a catalyst. Approximately 700 tons of silver are in continuous use in the production of plastics, for example.
- On that note, silver is necessary for producing soft plastics used in polyester textiles and is essential for producing a class of

plastics which includes adhesives, laminated resins for construction, plywood, and particleboard finishes.

- Silver is necessary for producing paper, electronic equipment, surface coatings, dinnerware, buttons, casings for appliances, handles and knobs, packaging materials, automotive parts, and electrical insulation materials.

- Silver is used for molded items, insulating handles for stoves, computers, electrical control knobs, and Mylar tape (which makes up 100 percent of audio, VCR and other types of recording tapes). It is also used to produce antifreeze.

- Silver is used in commemorative and proof coins around the world. There is wide silver use in silverware, jewelry, and the decorative arts.

- Silver is the best electrical conductor of all metals and is used in contacts and fuses and ordinary household wall switches.

- The use of silver for motor controls is universal in the home, and is even a better conductor of electricity than copper. Every time you turn on a microwave oven, a dishwasher, washing machine, dryer or TV set, you activate a switch with silver contacts. All electrical appliances, timers, thermostats, and some pumps, use silver contacts. Silver is also used for circuit breakers. A typical washing machine requires 16 silver contacts. A fully-equipped automobile may have more than 40 silver-tipped switches.

- A transparent coating of silver is used on double-paned thermal windows.

- Silver ions in house frames help resist mold and mildew.

- Silver relays are used in automobile accessories, vacuum cleaners, electric drills, elevators, escalators, machine tools, locomotives, marine diesel engines and oil-drilling motors. It is widely used for electrically-heated automobile windows and conductive adhesives.

- The majority of computers use silver-membrane switches. They are used for cable television, telephones, microwave ovens, learning toys, typewriter and computer keyboards, and in prepaid-toll gizmos. These silver-containing radio-frequency-identification devices will soon make an appearance embedded in credit cards and passports.

- Silver is used in circuit boards and is essential to electronics to control the operation of aircraft, car engines, electrical appliances, security systems, telecommunication networks, mobile telephones and TV receivers.
- Silver is used in windshields in General Motors all-purpose vehicles because it reflects some 70 percent of the solar energy. Every automobile produced in America has a silver ceramic line in the rear window to clear the frost and ice.
- Silver plating is used in Christmas tree ornaments, cutlery and hollow ware. Because it is virtually 100 percent-reflective after polishing, it is used in mirrors and coating for glass, cellophane, and metals.
- Silver has a variety of uses in pharmaceuticals and is widely employed as a bactericide and algaecide. Silver sulfadiazine is the most powerful compound for burn treatment worldwide. Catheters impregnated with silver diazine eliminate bacteria. Silver is increasingly being tapped for its bactericidal properties - from severe burns to wound-dressings to treating Legionnaire's Disease.
- Silver compounds are providing doctors with powerful clinical treatments against antibiotic-resistant bacteria. Silver ions have been used to purify drinking water and swimming pools for generations.
- One out of every seven pairs of prescription sunglasses incorporates silver.

Silver Photography

- Silver-based photography has superior definition and low cost. Photography is still the biggest consumer of silver. But is this changing with digital photography? Digital photography is considered by many to be a threat to old-fashioned film photography, as digital cameras are becoming the camera of choice for millions of people. Ergo, physical silver use will supposedly decline in the film business, and that is considered by many to be a bearish factor for silver. At one time, Kodak was the world's largest user of silver in manufacturing film. Their use of silver in every roll of film was touted as one reason for the silver bull market of the '70s.

There is a counterargument, and a counter-counterargument.

- It is not generally known, but much of the silver used in film is recycled and used again by the film companies. That is also true of the silver in medical x-rays.
- More than offsetting the above is the fact that silver is also used in glossy photographic print paper at Wal-Mart, Kmart, Costco, and other supermarkets for people to print out their digital photos. That paper is *never* recycled. One of my daughters informed me that now that she has a digital camera, she takes 12 times as many pictures of her boys as she did with her old-fashioned film camera, and she usually prints them out.

Regardless of the prevalence of digital cameras, the film companies will still sell one-billion rolls of film this year.

I could go on and on (I guess I already did), but it's apparent that these are all good reasons why our silver inventory is under assault. And if Butler is even partly right, silver could be turning into the supply/demand investment of the century.

Will the growing assault on silver inventories trigger a switch to some as-yet-unknown substitutes? In some cases, probably yes. Copper can do many of the things silver can do, but copper is rocketing up in price in a solid bull market and is becoming an increasingly expensive substitute. Usually, the amount of silver is so small in each of the individual units that incorporate it, that it is only a small part of the cost of manufacturing all the units. Therefore, there is not enough incentive to substitute raw materials at these prices, and collectively, they add up to thousands of tons of silver.

Silver as Money

Silver has an important monetary role, according to economic history. One disagreement I have with Butler is that he has discounted the monetary role of silver.

Silver has been consistently used as money throughout history, even more than gold, but as I have said several times before, whenever paper money fails (every 50 to 70 years), the world is subsequently littered with useless paper currencies. That's when silver is resurrected as money and comes back into its own.

For example, when the Chinese government fell at the end of World War II, they inflated the paper currency until it became distrusted, but almost like magic, silver and gold coins became the currency of choice all across that huge, primitive country. Everyone knew what an American silver dime was worth. This held true until the Communists imposed a new fiat currency and enforced it with the heavy hand of government.

Could that happen here in America? No one knows for sure, but that remote possibility is becoming less remote every day. You need some silver for insurance purposes because the dollar's fate seems to be sealed and delivered by our present rate of internal monetary inflation. Whether it takes one year, 10 years, or 30 years—I don't know exactly when— eventually the world will be littered with worthless paper dollars, and governments will be dragged kicking and screaming to a gold standard to back a new currency.

At some future time, silver coins will be minted again in massive quantities, and silver and gold will both reign triumphant over the world's monetary system. I don't know exactly how it will work, and probably nobody else does either. But for that reason, I repeat, you should buy at least one-half bag of junk silver (pre-1965 American dimes, quarters, and halves) for your family, just for the silver content.

Silver always rises during gold bull markets, usually twice as far and fast as gold, but the supply/demand situation (ETFs and jewelry and industrial usage) dwarfs all other reasons why silver will soar in price, perhaps much more than twice as much as gold.

The government coffers are now empty. In the '70s, Jimmy Carter announced they would be dumping some of the gold at Fort Knox into the market to depress the price, because rising gold was considered an embarrassment to the government. This time, Uncle Sam can't dump silver on the market to try to manipulate the price, or use their own inventory to make silver coins, because they don't have any. And they don't have a good reason to do so.

One other supply/demand factor that really matters is that COMEX has a monster silver futures exposure. I don't have the space to give you a complete dissertation on futures, but reread what I said about them earlier. And trust me on this–for every "long" contract there is a "short" contract. Many of the longs have bought a silver contract in the hopes that silver will be rising, and so will their contract. It can be settled either with a cash payment or by delivery of the physical metal. But a lot of the longs are silver users and need the metal. They have only bought the contracts for delivery and won't settle for cash, because they need the metal.

Warren Buffet, the legendary investor, bought 139-million ounces of silver via futures contracts eight years ago, and he demanded physical delivery. He had to sue to get it. He recently sold it, and just admitted he "sold too soon."

The shorts have sold silver they don't have, assuming they will be able to buy it back at a lower cost in the future and thereby profit handsomely. They are pure speculators, betting that the price will go down so they can buy it cheap. Steadily rising prices are their worst nightmare, and that's just what they got.

The "longs" needing delivery are more dangerous than the shorts. Remember, for every long contract, there is a corresponding short. As silver has soared, shorting losses have mounted to billions of dollars.

I guess the short speculators never learn. Back in the 70's, the zillionaire Hunt brothers tried to corner the silver market and drove the price from less than $2 to $50. Most of the governors of the COMEX were short, in effect betting against the Hunts. Their losses mounted day by day, and as they became more and more insolvent, their need to cover their shorts was far beyond their financial means. Technically the COMEX should have been shut down (as many of the shorts were governors of the COMEX) but shutting down the world's most important commodity exchange was unthinkable.

Eventually they won the battle with the Hunts by, among other things, changing the rules to "liquidation only." That's when I decided to tell my subscribers to sell their gold and silver at $35 an ounce, two weeks before the $50 top. When the elephants are fighting, we mice should scurry into the underbrush. Yes, it went to $50 for a few hours two weeks later, but close is good enough.

This is similar to where COMEX finds itself today. But this time, they are short so much silver that if they had to buy enough to cover all their shorts it could soak up as much as or more than 100 percent of all this year's silver production. Especially since many of the longs are users who need the physical silver for their industries and can't accept just a cash settlement. Also, the short's cash position is so dire, since their paper losses have mounted as silver has risen, that they may not have enough money for a cash settlement. Sooner or later, they will have to buy silver, and the stability price of silver could soon be above $100 an ounce (my best guess) in order to induce holders (you) to give up yours.

Silver is the investment of the century. It will move with gold, but further, as has already been demonstrated. Over the last couple of years gold is up about 100 percent, and silver is up more than 300 percent. We will eventually look back at silver at today's $12-$14 price as the bargain of the century. Silver and silver-mining stocks will be a license to print money.

My recommendations: For silver bullion coins or semi-numismatic coins, contact *Investment Rarities* by calling (800-328-1860), *International Collector's Associates* (800-525-9556), *Camino Coins* (800-982-7070), or *Kitco* (877-775-4826). Always compare prices. These are all dependable and time-tested. Prices may differ on any given day. You don't necessarily need the very cheapest, but close is good enough. I beg you on bended knee to buy silver! This is the safest investment call I have ever made.

CHAPTER 6

WHY WALL STREET
AND THE FINANCIAL MEDIA
HATE GOLD AND SILVER

*"No wonder governments don't like gold. No wonder
the central banks despise and fear gold. They fear gold
because when gold rises, it's telling the world that their
governments are debasing the currency."*

Richard Russell

all Street ignored gold and silver during most of the 1970's hyper-profitable bull market. They were either outright hostile or acted as though the metals didn't exist. I got no respect, even though my book (which sold three million copies) was near the top of *The New York Times* bestseller list for two years. I was all over the media—*Wall Street Week*, *Today*, *Regis and Kathie Lee*, etc,—and those hosts were often hostile, too. They all paid little attention to gold until it reached about $650 an ounce, far too late for them to have much of a chance for their clients to make money. In retrospect, we know that in 1979 the aging bull market was about to expire. It did soon after, following a brief climactic spurt to $850, then falling into a multi-year decline. They did their usual thing: they bought high, then held on too long and sold low.

Why the hostility? Partly because they believed their own rhetoric! Historically, rising gold always means falling stocks or a troubled world. They made most of their commissions in the stock market, thus remaining bullish on stocks and bearish on gold. Their bullish stock market recommendations were necessary because investors wouldn't buy stocks if their advisors were dubious about the market's future. They sneered at the inflation fears of us gold and silver fans, derisively called us gold investors "gold bugs." I didn't get any respect from Wall Street and didn't expect any, despite my book's success.

That's okay, because I have also lost much of my respect for them. I didn't receive any apologies when inflation soared to 18 percent, gold to $850, and silver to $50, and didn't expect any then either. Unfortunately, most of the young whippersnappers who now control Wall Street were in diapers 25 to 30 years ago during the last gold bull market, so they haven't experienced rising gold and inflation. Consequently, another gold bull market is inconceivable to them.

How about the media?

Studying "Psycho-ceramics"

I can't resist telling you about one of the funniest things that ever happened to me, illustrating the skepticism of mainstream media types regarding gold and silver. In 1978 I was on a national promotion tour for *How to Prosper During the Coming Bad Years* when I found myself in Detroit, rushing to a TV station for a scheduled interview on a big live morning show. I barely got there in time when the red light on the camera turned on. The host turned to the camera and said, "Today we're going to study *psycho-ceramics*, and with us today is a crackpot from California." The interview went downhill from there, with his biggest argument being that silver was an impractical investment for most people, unless you were very rich.

One year later, I found myself in the same studio, same host, promoting the mass paperback of my book. But this time, when the light went on, he said, "Today we have with us one of America's most brilliant financial advisors." After the show, I reminded him of what he had said before, and asked him what had changed his mind. He very sheepishly said, "I read your book and bought silver and tripled my money since you were here last." So the media is not hostile every time, but is usually wrong.

CHAPTER 6

Inside Wall Street

Let me explain to you how Wall Street works. It is a culture, as well as a financial institution.

Most of the young brokers, the big producers on Wall Street, are college graduates who have been trained in the stock market. In order to get the necessary advanced licenses to work there, they are trained in all the conventional investment vehicles and their relevant laws and regulations. Then they build their clientele based on the stock market. Commissions are how they make their money!

But they are all human beings, subject to all the errors of habit and behavior and peer pressure that plague all of us. They are surrounded by "group-think." They make tons of money on the status quo. I have visited firms on Wall Street with big trading rooms full of 20-something men and women whose annual income is measured in the millions–all from commissions on stock sales.

Few big Wall Street firms sell bullion (right offhand, I can't think of any, although the ETFs will probably change that), so it is money out of their pockets when hotshot brokers tell their big clients to sell some stock and put the money into bullion or coins. Maturity and client concern are scarce commodities on Wall Street.

When you meet these young brokers, you would be astounded at how money-oriented they are. They talk about their commissions and the things they buy with them. In their parking garage, I never saw so many Porsches, Lexuses and Mercedes. Too many brokers are bloodless mercenaries. And they are congenitally bullish on stocks, because that's where their bread is buttered.

Jim Dines is a case in point. At one time he was Wall Street's fair-haired boy. He had written the book on technical analysis which is still a classic, and his studies told him that we were moving into a stock bear market and a giant gold bull market. Not being reticent by nature, he made no secret of what he had concluded, and he went from fair-haired boy to outcast. It wasn't long before he and Wall Street had to part ways.

But Jim is the very definition of maverick, so he started one of the first gold newsletters and called himself "The Original Gold Bug." He was there before me (actually he has been there before me this time also). Jim and I became friends, and he was even a guest on my TV show, *Ruffhou$e*. I honor him as a real pioneer, and thank Wall Street for firing him. The newsletter business would be poorer without him. He is still publishing and well-worth reading (800-845-8259). He has a quirky life and is one of the bigger egos in a business that is loaded with big egos (like me). But he is a true professional, and an example of how Wall Street is so anti-gold. His newsletter is must-read for gold and silver and mining-stock investors (see Appendix A).

Financial Shows

Many of you listen to or watch financial shows. They are populated with guests who are typical examples of mainstream Wall Street financial thinking. The hosts and hostesses of the shows are steeped in the same traditions and attitudes. On the rare occasions when I am asked to be on such a show, I know that they are either ignorant of my real financial views or they are spoiling for a fight. Until gold and silver have risen so far they can't ignore them any longer, they will not be interested in guys like me. Until then, we gold and silver investors will be part of what amounts to an open underground movement, operating below the radar.

If your broker's opinion is important to you, you may be uncomfortable here. If you aren't a maverick, you had better become one, and be quiet about it. You will have to leave the herd, and for awhile, the herd is all on Wall Street.

Action Steps

If this book should persuade you to liquidate some of your stocks and buy some gold or silver or mining stocks, I suggest you don't tell your usual broker. If you do, you will be swimming upstream. You might want to open an account at Schwab where you will make your own decisions, and won't have to depend on a broker for approval. Or you can do business with *James Raby,* as we do (James Raby, *National Securities,* 800-431-4488). Jim is a walking encyclopedia on mining stocks (more in Chapter 11).

CHAPTER 7

GOLD, SILVER AND
THE PERFECT STORM

*"There is no means of avoiding the final collapse of a
boom brought about by credit expansion."*

Ludwig von Mises

Gold and silver can be useful in both a Best Case and a Worst
Case set of circumstances. Both of them will be immensely prof-
itable in very different ways, and the outlook is very different.
First let's investigate:

The Worst Cases: Terrorism and Other Things

The worst case is easy to describe. It means that terrible things have
happened that have changed the very nature of America and the world.
Let's consider just a few of the possible scenarios.

Less than five percent of the dollars in existence are actually minted
or coined. The rest are in cyberspace–in the computers of banks. The terrorists have enough money to hire the best hackers in the world, and
there is no computer system in the world that can't be hacked, given
enough time, money and talent. Where could Osama bin Laden get the
most bang for the buck? By destroying or corrupting the computers that
run the monetary system of the Western World.

He already attempted to do just that when he brought down the
World Trade Center. Fortunately, his intelligence was out of date. Until
about a year earlier many of those computers that control the monetary
system of the world were in the World Trade Center, but they had
recently been moved across the Hudson River to New Jersey, as well as

to Panama. Consequently, rather than the Western World's currency and bond markets being destroyed by the hideous blow, the markets were up and running in very few days with hardly a burp.

But there is an even more-deadly and less-risky alternative for bin Laden.

Panama and the Dollar

When we negotiated away the Panama Canal to Torrijos, the Panamanian dictator, our chief negotiator was Sol Linowitz, a member of the board of Chemical Bank in New York. He was appointed for one day less than six months, so his appointment would not be subject to congressional approval. Sure enough, the giveaway deal was signed one day before Linowitz' term was up.

One key part of Linowitz's banker-inspired mission was that the Canal Zone would be a "free-banking Zone," not subject to regulations or oversight. Even before the deal was signed, bank buildings were going up all over the Zone. Every multinational bank was there, and it appears that they moved many of the international money systems there, with no oversight or regulation. Who is to determine their safety or vulnerability? No one!

If terrorist hackers were to hack into those computers and infect them with a destructive virus, the entire dollar-based monetary system would disappear in a nanosecond. In that case, for all practical purposes, the only spendable money left would be gold or silver coins.

And what if they were able to sneak a nuke onto a ship and detonate it while in the canal? It's bad enough that the Chinese are in control of the ports on both ends of the canal. Imagine the chaos with the banks obliterated and commerce fatally crippled.

Or maybe they would only hack into the air traffic control system, indefinitely grounding every commercial plane in America—or into the North American power grid so your ATM or the electronically-operated cash registers at the supermarket wouldn't work. Wouldn't it be ironic if the monetary system of the world was brought down by some idiot-savant 17-year-old Al Qaeda-funded hacker, driven by money, ego, and political naivete??

Or what if terrorists managed to smuggle a nuclear weapon into the U.S. and detonate it, taking out the government, the Pentagon, or a few million people, throwing America into chaos, driving gold and silver into the stratosphere?

These and innumerable alternate scenarios may seem beyond the edges of credibility, but I dare you to say they are not possible.

This is not a forecast, only a speculation about a possible worst-case, we-hope-not scenario.

The Hyperinflation Scenario

What if monetary inflation reached a critical mass because of soaring demands on government (Medicare, Social Security, farm subsidies, pre-scription drugs, etc.) creating soaring deficits, and the subsequent inevitable consumer inflation rose until defensive consumer buying broke out into a real hyperinflation, with the modern money machine running night and day, like Germany during the 1920s? This would make money increasingly worthless and the precious metals increasingly precious. History tells us that this has happened over and over again, and we are repeating most of the same deadly mistakes.

But now we're not just talking about money. Let's pretend we are transported into a future where America is devastated by hyperinflation, and see what it looks like.

The world will be in terrible trouble, and the prosperity and comfort that you are familiar with will be in tatters. You will be surrounded by people struggling to survive, let alone prosper, as in the 1930s. That's what happened in Germany in the 1920s after the hyperinflation of the deutschmark, and the general suffering was the fertile ground which gave rise to Adolph Hitler. If you have prospered by holding gold and silver, you can buy a lot of safety and security while the country is being mended.

These are only a few of the possibilities. You can probably come up with better ones than I did. Share them with me, but don't give up hope! There is still:

The Best Case

Even if none of the worst-case scenarios ever happen and the currency system hangs together, monetary inflation has already been cooked into the economic cake by the Federal Reserve. *It is inconceivable to me*, given 31 years of studying and monitoring the economics of inflation, that the flood of "money" being poured into the world economy will *not* result in a ruinous inflation. If that doesn't happen, we will be making history. It will be the first time the money machines have run out of control where the result was not a ruinous, big-time inflation. Even in this "best-case" situation of an orderly world, you will make a bundle on this monetary-inflation-sensitive investment.

If all else fails, you can count on Social Security, Medicare and the prescription-drug program to trigger a flood of "money printing" and the subsequent monetary inflation, followed as night follows day with soaring-price inflation. As it becomes obvious to the public that these programs are plummeting into insolvency, the consumer inflation rate will soar, and so will gold and silver.

When the dire facts become obvious, Congress will start desperately searching for solutions, but which ones?

Will they raise taxes and watch FICA soar and taxpayers revolt? I doubt it.

Will they cut benefits or raise the Social Security retirement age? Maybe a little, but not much.

Will they dig in their heels and memorialize the current dysfunctional system by simply printing money? You bet! This will lay the groundwork for more ruinous inflation, and soaring gold and silver

In this best case (the most likely I think, I hope), we will at least see rising inflation and an inflationary recession, which is already written in cement. Gold and silver and their mining stocks can go up five to ten times, perhaps a lot more.

There is no best- or worst-case scenario in which I can conceive of gold and silver being losers. You can mortgage the kids and bet the farm! We can keep the odds decisively on our side!

CHAPTER 8

THE CLASSIC MIDDLE-CLASS INVESTMENT

"Inflation is always a monetary phenomenon, and the monetary phenomenon of the current era is one in which central banks around the world are increasing their money supplies. The rising price of gold is obviously reflecting this inflationary phenomenon."

Richard Russell

"I don't know enough about gold and silver, and I don't know where to go to get some," I hear you cry. I heard things like this many times during the last bull market. The mistaken assumption is that because metals-investing is not mainstream, that it must be complicated, or only for rich people, or hard for middle-class people of modest means. Nothing could be further from the truth. Let me address these problems one at a time.

• Buying and selling the metals is as easy as pie, and requires no more knowledge than you will get in this book. It's ideally suited for middle-class Americans. Gold and silver aren't just for rich, sophisticated people. Real estate and stocks and bonds require more than casual knowledge for you to be successful, but gold and silver are simplicity itself. You can walk into any coin dealer and walk out with your coins. Or you can buy them by phone or over the Internet from any of the national coin dealers that I recommend in this book and that my newsletter subscribers have safely done business with for many years. They are listed in the Appendix. They are honest and dependable, and you can compare their prices before you buy.

You can also buy shares of an ETF through any stock broker. It's as easy as buying mutual-fund shares. ETFs are explained in Chapter 5 and Chapter 11.

• Gold and silver coins are a lot cheaper than the stock market, where you have to buy in round lots of 100 shares (as much as $25,000) to get a decent price, or have gobs of money just to open an account. If you want to buy mining stocks through our recommended mining-stock dealer, Jim Raby (800-431-4488), he will accept accounts with as little as $5,000.

You can buy a roll of U.S. silver dimes (pre-1965) for around $50 as of this date, and a one-ounce gold coin (a krugerrand or American gold eagle) for between $600 and $700. Or you can buy a half-bag of junk silver coins for around $4,500 as of this date.

Gold and Silver in the Ground

If you choose to buy gold and silver in the ground in the form of mining stocks, things get a bit more complicated, but no more than picking any stock. I will cover this in much more detail in Chapter 11, but I would like to cover a few basics here, because these stocks will be at least twice as profitable as coins or bullion.

Mining stocks are simpler than most stocks in one respect—all the stocks in this industry group will rise when the metals go up. Remember, when the wind blows, even the turkeys fly. You just have to watch one thing: the price of the metals. Although, there can be special factors for you to be aware of when picking the best stocks. That is what *The Ruff Times* is for.

Mining stocks all have one special advantage. When Congress authorized tax-free savings programs, like IRA's and 401k's, they banned bullion from these investment instruments by law. They limited them to securities and American gold coins since they didn't want to make it harder for the Treasury to sell their gold and silver eagles. You may have trouble getting the trustee of your IRA or 401k to allow you to buy eagles or mining stocks, but the law permits it, so you may need to change trustees, or switch to another management company. But securities can always legally be put into a self-directed plan.

In the long run, mining stocks are no harder to buy and sell than any other class of stocks. They have been booming for a couple of years now, and some of the big, well-run mines are listed in *The Wall Street Journal.*

The Dart-board Method

The biggest problem is choosing which stocks to buy. Jim Raby will have some suggestions, and so do I. In the Appendix and in Chapter 11, you will find a list of OK mining stocks. Put all of their names on a piece of paper, put them on the wall and throw ten darts at them. Then invest in the holes. You will have created your own personal mutual fund.

As crazy as this sounds, the dart-board approach has a lot of advantages. It gives you diversity. All your eggs will not be in one basket. You don't know which stocks will be the biggest winners, but as time goes on, some will perform better than others, and you can weed out the laggards and concentrate your money on the winners.

To monitor the metals every day as I do, just check the free website of *Kitco* (a recommended bullion and coin dealer) at www.kitco.com/charts/livegold.html.

All in all, we fear the unknown, but it won't take long to get to know the metals as old friends. The only hang-ups you will have are when you are told by your broker that this is a bad idea. He is wrong, dead wrong!

CHAPTER 9

SHRINKING SUPPLY, RISING DEMAND

*"If SLV approaches anything close to the popularity of the
other ETFs, then silver's run-up may be more spectacular
than anyone can imagine."*

Texas Hedge Report

N ow it's time for Ruffonomics 101.

It has truly been said that if you lined up all the world's economists in a row, they still couldn't reach a conclusion. But one thing they would all agree on is the immutable law of supply and demand. It can't be repealed, and we will never see a prolonged gold and silver bull market without the supply/demand situation first being in our favor.

Here's how it works: when demand for a commodity or service declines and the supply rises, the price falls. These are the ingredients of a bear market To the contrary, when supply falls or remains stable and demand rises, the price rises and you have a bull market. The element that brings them into balance is price. Thus endeth the lesson.

The gold and silver supply/demand situation is now heavily in our favor, with supply falling and demand rising, and there are reasons why this will not change for years. Here's why.

Falling Supply

During the discouraging 22-year bear market, gold and silver miners were faced with a huge dilemma. The metals' prices had fallen to the point that miners had to sell them below the cost of production, so most of the producers pulled in their horns. They slashed their exploration and production budgets, and sat on their hands to wait for a better day. And their stocks fell and fell as their earnings withered. Many of them came close to going broke.

But they couldn't just shut down, they had to sustain their infrastructure. Some gold companies hedged their bets by selling their future production on the futures market so they wouldn't lose money as the price fell. *Barrick*, the biggest gold producer, is a striking case in point. Near the bottom of the bear market, in a classic case of bad timing, they sold their future production for $350 an ounce for years to come. It was a huge bet on falling prices, and they lost the bet. To their horror, gold has been in a bull market-currently selling for around $700 an ounce. As the price has gone up, their hedging losses have mounted, and they have done their best to legally hide those losses in small-print footnotes on their balance sheet.

Barrick's stock hasn't yet been hurt, as their hedging losses have escaped notice. Barrick has risen with the rest of the industry. As a result, Barrick will be behind some of the better performers when all the results are in.

Barrick has recently acquired another giant company and as a result is now the world's largest gold producer, but will be weighed down by its former hedging policy.

Silver's Status

On the supply side, there is always some silver production, as it is also a byproduct of mining other metals. For instance, because silver is a byproduct of copper mining, and sometimes other metals, that means that as long as there is copper mining, there will always be some silver production. That is why I recommend *Phelps Dodge*, one of the world's largest copper miners. (More about them in Chapter 11). They are an especially good bet because copper is also in a bull market, and the price of silver has so far had relatively little effect on Phelps' earnings. Because their real profits are in copper, they can just sell their silver at the current market price and it is all incremental income.

On the demand side, China and India are teeming with newly-minted capitalists and middle-class investors who are pouring a lot of their new-found wealth into gold and silver jewelry and investments. Companies like Wal-Mart are sending them billions to pay for the cheap goods we are buying at Wal-Mart's superstores.

Actually, it won't take much money going into metals or mining stocks to move the markets. If you add up the dollar value of all the gold and silver supplies in existence, plus the market value of all the stocks of the mining companies, it would total far less than the market capitalization of Google or Microsoft. As important as it is, gold is a comparatively tiny market at this price. A relatively small amount of buying has a disproportionate effect on the price

But as I discussed in Chapter 5, silver is affected by demand factors that gold isn't because of its unique status as an industrial metal. Because the supply side of the equation is written in cement, rising demand will move silver.

As the price rises and silver has become profitable to produce, miners have stepped up their exploration and production, but they have two problems: 1) their best efforts cannot keep up with demand; and 2) it will take them four to ten years to get a new mine into production. So the supply/demand situation is sharply in the favor of investors and speculators for some years to come.

This is a supply/demand grenade which is only waiting for investors to wake up to the inexorable math before gold hits more than $2,000 and silver explodes over $100.

CHAPTER 10

GOLD AND SILVER SCAMS AND HOW TO DODGE THEM

G old has always been an attractive lure for scam artists in every metals bull market when enthusiasm is growing. The scam artists are well aware of the emotional appeal of gold, so this is where they are most active. Also, because it is not part of the usual investment world, they can play upon the ignorance of gold and silver investors, especially since it attracts a lot of those who haven't invested in public markets before. Taking unfair advantage of the bull market, especially in the case of older novices, becomes immensely lucrative.

In the last gold and silver bull market during the '70s, scam artists oozed out of the woodwork. They had an armory of different strategies: They promised to finance gold or silver on margin to double (or more) your profits; they offered to store your gold, and then they disappeared–with the gold! In the current bull market, history will teach us again the hard lesson that there will be myriad scams. A scam artist's ingenuity knows no bounds. In the past, I have exposed some of those attractive scams that saved thousands of potential investors millions of dollars.

I learned one lesson the hard way, and so did some of my subscribers. In the 80s, I founded Ruffco, a coin and bullion dealer. Eventually I sold it, but unbeknownst to me, the buyer turned out to be a crook and was eventually convicted and confined at Nellis Federal Prison in Nevada. His crime? After he bought the company from me, he took the metal that my trusting subscribers had put into Ruffco's storage program, sold it, and kept the money for himself. I feel a sense of accountability, and when I have enough resources to deal with the large amounts of money involved, I intend to do my best to make those people whole. I'm not sure I can do it fully, but I will really try.

Scams are, by their very nature, usually conducted by articulate, bright sales people. Some of them can talk the birds out of the trees. When they get a potential "mark" on the telephone, they are immensely skilled at sounding legitimate and selling you on the idea. After all, they are salesmen for a scam, and they are often very good at it.

The most-important rule is very simple: *if you buy something over the phone from someone you don't know, you are probably making an unsecured loan to a crooked stranger!* The scam artists will be renting phone numbers and launching their pitch, and you might be on that list.

These scams usually fit into the following categories:

- **Gold sales and storage scams.** They will sell you the metal and then contract to store it, but the storage facility will be empty. Back in the 70s, I happened to visit a storage unit in a cave in the Wasatch Mountains. While I was touring the facility, I saw the area that was rented to one major bullion firm that I had never recommended. Out of curiosity, I looked it over and found only a few gold coins. I knew they were doing business in the millions, and, according to the propaganda, they had stored millions of dollars worth of gold in this secure facility buried in this cave. When I realized the cupboard was bare, I immediately contacted Dan Rosenthal, publisher of *The Gold and Silver Report*, and the two of us simultaneously published the exposé. Unfortunately, the people who had already lost money had no legal loss claim under a quirk in the law. Pursuing it was love's labor lost.

The sure protection is to *never store your metals with the seller, unless it is a well-established Wall Street firm, appropriately insured and regulated,* preferably with a trust fund and an independent trustee so you are protected.

When you buy large amounts of gold or silver bullion bars, there is one advantage in storing them with the seller. When you sell it, you won't have to submit the metals for an assay, which is time consuming and sometimes expensive. For this reason, buying bullion coins and taking them home is the safest way to do it. But if you have a lot of money, all things being equal, there are advantages to buying bullion and storing it. Just be sure the storage firm has a long track record beyond reproach, and you have an independent trustee. Buyer beware!

- **Margin buying.** Many of the crooked sellers (and even some of the more-or-less legal ones) will hire commission salesmen to pitch you on buying several times as much metal with your money by buying "on margin." That means that if you decide to order $1,000 worth of gold or silver, they will suggest that, instead, you put down your $1,000 as a down payment and buy on five or 10 or 20 percent margin. They will loan you the balance, so you can buy five to 10 times as much gold or silver. That means you could buy as much as $10,000 worth of bullion with the same amount of money that would have bought you $1,000 worth of fully-owned metal. Very attractive! Then they will charge you exorbitant interest on the loan

The hazards are monumental! In the first place, if gold should have one of its periodic temporary bull-market declines while on the way up, it could wipe out the value of your margin, and the margin lender will take care of himself first. He will give you a "margin call," which means you need to put up more cash or be liquidated.

Another rule is simple; *never* meet a margin call!

If you buy on margin, you can make up to 10 times as much money if the metal goes up, but you can lose 100 percent of your money if the metal nosedives far enough to wipe out your margin and force you to put up more cash or sell out at a loss. Bad or unlucky timing can devastate you. And this doesn't even take into account the huge commissions these sharpies take out of your money at some of these highly-marketed firms.

Also, some of these margin sellers are running a double scam–they are not only selling you the gold or silver on margin, but supposedly "storing" it. When they combine the appeal of the margin pitch with the alleged convenience of storage, it is immensely seductive. Don't respond. Hang up! One thing I have done when I get one of those calls is to ask them to call me on my business number. Then I give them the number of my local Consumer Protection office.

I'm sure that the scam artists will come up with more ways to part you from your money if you show an interest in gold or silver. Stick with the merchants that we have recommended. That doesn't mean the others are necessarily bad, but these are the dependable ones with long histories. They can be trusted.

The key to success is that when you leave the Wall Street investment mainstream, be sure you land in a safe boat on the gold and silver mainstream. Those dealers who kept the faith during the barren years for decades or longer are the people with whom to do business.

CHAPTER 11

MINING STOCKS: A LICENSE TO PRINT MONEY

N ow let's get just a bit more sophisticated in our pursuit of profits. History has shown us that in a metals bull market you will
make a lot more money in silver than you will in gold, but you
will make more than twice as much money in selected gold and silver
mining stocks as you will in silver. Why? Because they are uniquely
leveraged in relation to pure bullion. More about that in a moment.

I have prepared this chapter with the indispensable help of James
Raby of *National Securities* (800-431-4488). Jim is a consummate pro, and
he has forgotten more about mining stocks than you and I will never
know. On second thought, I take that back; I don't think he has forgotten anything! The typical stockbroker knows little or nothing about
mining stocks, and is often forbidden by his company to trade Canadian
stocks. Raby trades both in Canada and the U.S.

Some of the best capital-gains possibilities are young companies
listed only in Canada. The symbols include **T, TO** (the Toronto
Exchange) or **V** or **TV** (Toronto Ventures, the old Vancouver Exchange,
now a subsidiary of Toronto). If your broker can't do business in
Canada, you will miss out on some of the greatest speculative opportunities, where the long-term return might be 1,500 percent or more,
as opposed to 500 percent.

Often the first listing of a publicly-traded mining company is in
Canada. As more is known through the development process, they will
graduate from Canada to the Bulletin Board in the U. S., then perhaps
to NASDAQ, then to the American Exchange with the cost of admission
getting progressively higher.

The Genesis of a New Mining Company

All mining companies have to start somewhere, and it might be helpful for the new investor to understand their origins.

To make money in the mining business, you have to invest in good people; the better and more experienced the people, the better the odds that they will locate and acquire good properties. The properties are usually hundreds if not thousands of acres.

Once the prospective property is found, they start the soil sampling and trenching in hopes that the results they get back from the lab are positive enough that these assays merit a drill program. Drilling these targets can be very costly and requires a lot of money and time.

If the drill program is successful, meaning good results are realized from the initial drilling, then additional capital is raised and additional drilling is done until a "resource" is discovered. More capital is raised and extensive drilling continues until the drill-indicated reserve becomes large enough to be considered an "orebody." Ore in *miner's term,* means "profit."

Next comes a "feasibility study." Then, quite often, a major mining company will take an interest and conduct their own feasibility studies to decide if they want to invest in or buy the project to replenish their reserves. As good news comes in, the price of the stock moves up, but conversely, the leverage for investors decreases. The more you are willing to risk early in the game when less is known, the lower the price, and the bigger your possible gains. Conversely, the more extensive the improvements, the more likely the price will be higher, thus a lower opportunity for large gains. Companies in the Development stage, especially those still listed in Canada, offer a unique opportunity to literally get in on the ground floor.

Investors in Exploration and Development stocks will take more risks with their money, but the upside can be astronomical. Possible huge returns are what draw people into the junior-mining sector, even though these properties can take years to become producing mines.

Leverage

Now let's look at the leverage that is routinely found in a gold or silver mine. Let's do the math. Follow me carefully, because this is the key to understanding why you will make a lot more money in a gold or silver bull market than you would in just bullion.

Let's assume you own some gold bullion at $350 an ounce, and gold goes to $400. Your $50 profit (at least on paper) is about 14 percent.

But now, let's assume you are *a shareholder of a mining company* that produces gold at $300 an ounce and gold is now at $350. The mine is currently making $50 an ounce on every ounce it produces, but if gold goes to $400, they are now making $100 an ounce. The profits have doubled! That's a 100 percent increase in profitability, so your stock probably will at least double!

That's 100 percent-plus, compared to 14 percent! That's about seven-times better! Historically, a development or exploration company that strikes it rich may eventually give you 15 or 20 times as much profit as bullion. That's why I said that mining stocks may be like a license to print money!

There is one caveat: although mining stocks should do well all through the bull market, history tells us they will probably give us the biggest returns nearer to the climactic blow-off. They will require a lot of patience, so buy now, put them away, and hang on for several years

The Mining Stock Pyramid

There is a strategy I call, "playing the pyramid." Early in the bull market, the first stocks to rise will be the blue chips at the top of the pyramid with low production costs. Many of those companies are so big that when they open a new mine, this will have less impact on profits than a smaller company might enjoy from a new mine.

As gold rises, you can move down the pyramid to shares of the higher-cost or smaller- production companies that have just become profitable as the price of gold rises above their profit threshold. This gives you more leverage, as a five percent move in gold could mean as much as a 100 percent increase in mining profits and a big run up in their stock.

As this book is written, the best speculative opportunities are moving down the pyramid to the smaller-production and higher-cost producers.

You can, in effect, start at the top with the biggest, most stable producers and work down. You should probably start with *Newmont* (NEM-NYSE).

As you move down the pyramid, both the risk and the potential profit increase.

Another strategy is to diversify across the whole spectrum from top to bottom. Then as the market matures over time, shift the weight of your allocation towards the bottom of the pyramid–the exploration and development companies.

Also, a gold or silver strike, or the acquisition of a development company with proven reserves, can have a greater impact on the production and profits of small to medium producers than it would on a giant blue chip mining company. It will be a windfall for both the shareholders of the acquired company and the acquiring company. Holding the shares of an acquisition target can be a huge windfall. I'll keep up on the potential merger deals, and report on them.

Silver mining stocks should be the stars.

Big changes will occur as the market matures. There will be many acquisitions, mergers and barren holes, as well as upside surprises. I will keep you posted in *The Ruff Times* (877-665-6818, www.rufftimes.com), and will also have links to some other writers (as listed in Appendix A) who can give you additional enlightenment on the market and other choices in addition to what I have offered here.

Here are the major categories. Some of them cross the lines, so I'll do the best I can. To avoid going down deep and coming up dry, I have included only a partial list in this small book. This list is not a "portfolio," but an a la carte menu for you to choose from–a selected, limited list, and a moving target. It is as the market is now. A year from now this list will be partially obsolete. I will stay abreast of the changes and continually publish an expanded and revised list in *The Ruff Times*, especially in the Development and Exploration categories.

I have included here only those which are most likely to still be on the menu a year from now.

Mutual Funds

If you put the shares of a metals mutual fund in your IRA or 401k, you can legally circumvent the ban on bullion in tax-favored savings instruments. In fact, that's true of all stocks. Funds which invest in mining shares should all perform well with varying degrees of success, and there is an active market for all of them. If you really want to diversify, you can buy more than one.

ASA LTD (ASA). A closed-end fund, owning mostly South African mining shares. Because of the deteriorating political and social situation in South Africa, I don't like it as well as the other choices.

Central Fund of Canada Ltd. (CEF). Listed on the American Exchange. It is a pure bullion fund and maintains a ratio of 50 ounces of silver to one ounce of gold. It is a near perfect proxy for bullion which cannot usually be held in an IRA or other tax-protected plan, like you can with CEF. However, the new gold and silver ETFs may make CEF obsolete, as now you can buy shares of each metal in whatever ratio you prefer. The gold/silver ratio may narrow to as little as 20-to-one in the future, making silver even more profitable than gold. I will report on the current ratio in *The Ruff Times*.

American Century Global Gold (BGEIX). An open-end, no-load mutual fund, which probably has the lowest expense ratios.

Tocqueville Gold (TGLDX). An open-end, no-load mutual fund.

US Global Investors (USERX): An open-end, no-load mutual fund.

Fidelity Select Gold (FSAGX). An open-end mutual fund.

ETFs (Exchange-traded Funds)

ETFs are traded on major exchanges, and are a lot like mutual funds, except where mutual funds are only traded at the end of the market day when the price has "settled," ETFs can be bought or sold at any time of the trading day, just like any other stock. They are an easy way to invest in gold and silver bullion, and will open up the metals for more traditional investors, moving bullion into the much-bigger middle-class market. They are immensely bullish for the metals.

The silver ETF is *iShares Silver Trust* (SLV). The gold ETF is *Streettracks Gold Trust* (GLD).

Some people in the precious metals newsletter industry are worried over whether or not the funds will really buy the physical metal, rather than "proxies" like gold or silver mining stocks, when new investors send them money. The sponsoring firms (such as Barclays) are too substantial and too regulated to try something fraudulent like that, but I will monitor this just in case.

Political Risk

This is not the conventional gold bug wisdom, but I am a bit concerned with political risk in the undeveloped world. As exploration has gone farther afield, more and more of these companies are in places like primitive Africa, China, Vietnam, and South America. These companies are only as sound as their relations with sometimes-volatile governments.

Recently, for instance, Chavez, the Marxist madman who runs Venezuela, has just seized control of the American oil companies operating in his country. The newly-elected president of Bolivia has just nationalized all the foreign gas companies doing business there (incidentally, I am told that Chaves owns the chain of Citgo gas stations, so when you buy gas at Citgo, you may be putting money into Chavez' pocket).

Is this the wave of the future for mining companies? I don't know, but as they become more profitable, they will be very tempting targets for expropriation. When Bolivia made their announcement, the stock of Apex Silver, which has Bolivian holdings, took a beating for a day or two because of concern over the future.

For that reason, I would assign a smaller portion of my portfolio to companies with big operations in potentially unstable countries, and concentrate most of my money on companies with American and Canadian mines, and there are plenty of them. Don't ignore the foreign companies completely, just be a bit more cautious.

I have placed an asterisk next to the name of the companies with more than 50% of their operations or production in North America.

CHAPTER 11

Blue Chips: The Major Gold Producers

(These are companies with annual production of more than one-million ounces.) The list of blue chips could even begin and end with *Newmont* (NEM-NYSE). It's one of the biggest producers, is stable, and tends to be among the first movers when a bull market is getting under way.

Other big gold producers I like are *Gold Fields* (GFI), **Goldcorp* (GG), *Freeport McMoran* (FCX), **Kinross* (KGC) and *Anglo Gold* (AU)

Second-Tier Producers

(These are a few of the companies producing annually between 50-thousand and one-million ounces.)

*Agnico Eagle (AEM), *Bema* (BGO), **Cambior* (CBJ) and *Glamis* (GLG)

Development Companies

(These are mining companies that have found an ore body and are further defining it by drilling, etc. Some have proven reserves in the ground. They are often shopping for a big partner to finance their development, or even to sell out to them.)

*Alamos (AGI), *Arizona Star* (AZC), *Crystallex* (KRY), **Farallon* (FAN) and **Miramar* (MNG)

Exploration Companies

(Exploration companies are at the bottom of the pyramid and are looking for properties to acquire, explore and develop.)

Golden Arrow (GRG-V), *US Gold* (USGL), **Dejour* (DJE-V), **Rubicon* (RBY) and *Madison* (MMR-V)

There is an additional assortment in *The Ruff Times* that in my not-so-humble opinion, are also worthy of attention, although I am sure there are other fine companies. I believe this category may be the biggest winner when the last dog is hung. Some of them are in my personal portfolio. You can put this list on your dartboard as described later.

Pure Silver-Mining Companies

These stocks will especially be like a license to print money:

I like *Hecla* (HL) (a giant), *Pan American Silver* (PAAS), *Silver Wheaton* (SLW), *Silver Standard* (SSRI), and *Coeur D'Alene Mines* (CDE). There are several others noted in *The Ruff Times*.

Combination Plays

Phelps Dodge (PD), one of the world's largest copper mines, is also a big silver producer. You can benefit with Phelps from the ongoing massive bull market in copper, as well as in silver. Because their expenses are all covered by copper mining, the silver that comes along as a byproduct is essentially without any cost and represents profit for the company.

Another especially interesting one is *Northern Dynasty Minerals, Ltd.* (NAK). They are located in Alaska, and have an estimated 18 billion pounds of copper, and 15-20 million ounces of gold. I own some Dynasty.

More Advice

Not all management teams have the same degree of qualification, experience and integrity. My job, with the help of experts I trust, is to help sort out the sheep from the goats so you can make good picks, but it is foolish to try to decide which mine will be the best performer. I'm not smart enough to do that. But remember, "a rising tides raises all boats," and I will do my best to sort out the real winners. The cream will rise to the top, although early in the game, the scum also rises. The cream will remain, and the scum will dissipate.

I suggest you start your own small mutual fund by making a list of my recommended mining companies (especially the Development and Exploration companies), posting the list on a dart board on the wall, throwing ten darts at it, and then dividing the money up among the holes. As you gather more experience over time, you will see which stocks are performing the best, and then you can prune your list and concentrate your money in three or four of the best ones. The odds are that they will all rise, but not equally. The key is to spread your risk, then shift your money to the winners.

Not too long ago I spoke at a gold investment conference in San Francisco, and the exhibit hall was loaded with small mining companies looking for investors. They all had great stories. If you go to one of these conferences, make a list of the exhibiting companies and use my dart-board method. Never try to pick just one given mine.

There is much to learn, but they are as easy to buy as any stock because they are generally listed over-the-counter or on an exchange. Some of the less-mature stocks are listed on the Toronto Ventures exchange (the old Vancouver Exchange). Many blue chip mining stocks are also listed on the American or New York Stock Exchanges and you can track them every day in *The Wall Street Journal.*

This category can be loaded with opportunity, with picks ranging from conservative to highly speculative. Sometimes the first stocks to move are not necessarily the best ones, just the ones with the best PR and marketing. We will try to steer clear of those. Some of the best will be laggards for a while because they are more concerned with running a mining company and doing sound exploration and drilling than they are with cultivating investors. Sometimes they are well financed and have worked out partnership deals with major companies. Sooner or later the world will discover them and they will outperform many of the early winners.

This is an immensely profitable game. But don't forget that your safest course of action will be to buy gold and silver coins and take them home. You should buy gold and silver in the ground *only* after you have taken care of your insurance and basic investment positions with coins and bullion. But of course, that is all up to you. If you are a novice at the mining-stock game, start conservatively with the giants, like *Newmont,* *Hecla* and *Phelps Dodge.*

But remember, as your growing knowledge adds to your confidence, mining stocks in this gold and silver bull market may be your once-in-a-lifetime chance to get sincerely rich investing.

CHAPTER 12

INCOME IN A GOLD BULL MARKET

Many of my readers are retired or widows and need regular income from their investments. How can you get income when you have bought into my vision and converted your savings into hard assets, rather than interest-yielding bonds, utility stocks or other mature, dividend-paying stocks? And should you do that?

The usual Wall Street counsel for retired older people is to buy "conservative" bonds or dividend-paying blue-chip stocks. In fact, now that many Wall Street advisors are apparently concerned about the immediate future of the stock market, especially "growth stocks," they are going back to the old standby—"shift more of your holdings into more conservative investments," like bonds.

No, no, no!!

Bonds are an especially *bad* idea in a time of rising interest rates, and rates will be rising for the foreseeable future. But why are bonds such a bad idea?

- You shouldn't lock yourself into low bond yields when rates are rising. If you do, in the future, you will look with envy on those who waited and are getting higher rates.

- When interest rates rise, the market value of bonds goes down, and that is also true of any fixed-return investment. What you gain in income will be more than offset by capital losses. In the '70s, I watched as rates climbed above 18 percent, and bonds (even super-safe T-bonds) lost half of their market value, and so did dividend-paying stocks.

So what's to be done? There are several alternatives, some of them very unorthodox.

- **Buy shares of a money-market fund for future income as rates rise**. Money-market funds are mutual funds that invest strictly in short-term securities, like short-term Treasury bills that mature in a month or less. Sometimes they even buy overnight bank securities. The fund managers will turn over their whole portfolio in a month or less, reinvesting them at higher yields as rates rise. The law requires that they pass the yields on to you, and maintain shares at the same price. They are as close to being as free of risk as you can find in this risky world. In the '70s, I was one of the first to advise and teach my followers about money-market funds, as few had even heard of them.

The neat thing is that you can withdraw your funds at any time by simply writing a check against them. You got the yields of a bank CD with the liquidity of a low-yielding demand deposit. In the '70s, interest rates rose continually for years. At one time, my subscribers were getting as much as 18 percent.

- **Use a money-market fund rather than a no-yield to low-yield bank checking account**. Don't get sucked into a bank "money-market account." They are the banks' reaction to the competition of legitimate money-market funds. They are not the same. They are merely bank deposits competing badly with higher yields than they used to pay before they were forced to compete. They are usually just CDs masquerading as money-market funds, complete with the deceptive label. In the '70s, rates rose to as high as 18 percent. The same thing should happen in this bull market. Rates are low now, as this is written, but they will rise, and soon

- **Here is an oddball idea** that flies in the face of conventional wisdom. *You can sell off say 8 percent, or whatever you need, of your gold or silver coins or mutual-fund shares each year for income.* This strategy has several advantages. If I am right about the bull market in the metals, the remaining coins will appreciate faster than your withdrawal. Your capital will keep growing. Also, you will be paying the capital-gains-tax rate, rather than the higher personal income tax rate you would be paying on bond interest.

If you choose the coin-selling strategy, you should own an assortment of various-sized gold and silver coins and semi-numismatics to make it convenient. I will be writing more about smaller oddball coin sizes in the future.

Big Yields in Canada

• **Canadian oil and gas funds** have been paying nine to 15 percent annually. With the soaring price of crude oil, natural gas and gas at the pump, this should continue into the foreseeable future. The list includes:

CompanyYield

ADVANTAGE ENERGY INCOME FUND (AVN'U-T)13.7 percent
BAYTEX ENERGY TRUST (BTE'U-T)10 percent
ENERPLUS RESOURCES FUND (ERF)9.3 percent
PARAMOUNT ENERGY TRUST (PMT'U-T)14.4 percent

These stocks have several advantages as the price of oil climbs. Not only will the dividend increase with rising oil prices, but there is a capital-gains kicker: as the stocks will also go up with rising oil, the dividend will increase as the subsequent rising profits are passed onto you.

These trusts are designed as income investments. The companies take only as little as one percent of the profits, and the rest is paid out in dividends. They are a great investment. Current yields will change daily, so call Jim Raby at National Securities (800-431-4488) for the latest quotes. I have no financial interest in your transactions with Raby. You're welcome.

Several other income producers will be discussed in *The Ruff Times* from time to time.

CHAPTER 13

SEMI-NUMISMATIC COINS

Most people think there are only two kinds of gold and silver coins–bullion coins and "numismatic" or "rare" coins. I spoke with Chuck Helvig and Drew Crowell, the research and semi-numismatic directors of *International Collectors Associates* (800-525-9556) to understand the field and get their help in gathering information for this chapter.

***** *****

Numismatic coins are not a subject for this book—they are legal-tender coins that were minted a long time ago and exist only in very limited supply. They are eagerly sought after by collectors, and their value is based strictly on their rarity, age, condition and demand. The current price of gold plays little or no part in the price of each numismatic coin, and the premiums are far higher than that of bullion coins. Grading is also more subjective. Most rare numismatic coins are purchased in higher grades such as "MS-66" or "MS-70," which includes very-rare, museum-quality U.S. and foreign gold coins.

But in between the extremes of common bullion coins and numismatics is an interesting category: *semi*-numismatic coins. They are not as rare or expensive as numismatic coins, and they generally range in condition from "circulated" to "MS-65." Commissions are very low compared to numismatic coins. They are very liquid, just like bullion, and there is always a two-way market. They have a high-bullion content, are priced much closer to the bullion content than numismatic coins, and offer the same privacy that numismatic coins offer.

Dealer Reporting

Most investment assets are highly visible, traceable, and reportable and watched by the government. With the new cash- and metals-transaction reporting laws and regulations, even cash, cashier's checks, money orders and most forms of gold are reportable. In fact, the privacy which was guaranteed by the Constitution's Fourth Amendment has, for the most part, disappeared as far as investments are concerned.

When you sell bullion coins to a coin dealer, the dealer is required by law to report that sale to the IRS on Form 1099. That is one handicap with bullion coins. However, there is an exemption for rare coins which covers *semi-numismatics*. Coins with a premium of more than 15 percent do not have to be reported by a coin dealer when they buy yours. The $20 Liberty and the $20 St. Gaudens coins have a premium higher than 15 percent and are outside of dealer-reporting requirements.

Everyone should own some assets that no one else knows about, which are low-profile, bearer-type investments that leave no tracks. Semi-numismatic coins fit this bill.

Protecting Against Confiscation

Unfortunately, many governments have a history of confiscating gold bullion coins. Although I am not terribly concerned about this issue as explained in Chapter 14, it needed to be addressed. But even if there is confiscation, one type of gold exempt from this draconian measure is "gold coins having a recognized special value to collectors of rare and unusual coins." In other words, numismatic and semi-numismatic gold coins.

Since 1975, you have been allowed to own gold bullion and gold bullion coins. But during some future crisis, politicians may possibly make gold illegal and confiscate gold bullion bars and coins. It is highly unlikely, and probably impossible to implement so I don't spend a lot of time considering this, but it is possible. The semi-numismatic coins would be exempt from such confiscation if history is a guide.

You might consider U.S. circulated silver dollars. Circulated silver-dollar bags contain 1,000 circulated U.S. silver dollars, most of which are more than 75 years old. They offer investor-grade anonymity because they are not reported. They are considered collectibles and are less likely to be confiscated. They also offer the investor a double play on both the silver content and the scarcity of the coin.

Each bag of dollars contains approximately 770 ounces of silver. They can be purchased in bags of 1,000 coins or in fractional bags of 500, 250 or 125 silver dollars. If you want an upscale semi-numismatic silver dollar with fine investment potential, certified 'MS-63" to "MS-65" U.S. silver dollars fill the bill. In the past, they have traded from five to 10 times above their current level. Also, rolls (20 coins) of "MS-60" Morgan and Peace silver dollars are popular and profitable. Remember my bias in favor of silver.

Before buying semi-numismatic coins, there are some things you need to ask:

- Is the coin protected from confiscation? Semi-numismatic coins fill that bill as described above. Only five percent of all the gold in the U.S. is in collectible coins, so it is simply not worth the government's effort to confiscate every coin collection.
- Will the coins help protect your privacy? We have already covered this. The sale of numismatic or semi-numismatic coins to a coin dealer is not reportable to the IRS by the dealer as long as their collectible premium above the bullion value is above 15 percent.
- Is the coin dealer reputable? We have recommended three semi-numismatic coin dealers: *International Collector's Associates* (800-525-9556), *Investment Rarities* (800-328-1860), and *Camino Coins* (800-982-7070). If you stick with these, you will be safe.

Semi-numismatic coins should be part of your portfolio because of their safety, investment potential and low premium. Semi-numismatic coins are interesting because they have more bullion than most rare coins, and consequently, a floor on the price, which is the current price of bullion. They are a convenient way to invest in gold and silver, with the added bonus of some scarcity value.

Most of the reputable dealers, including those I have listed, are concentrating a lot of their customer sales effort on semi-numismatic coins. There are good reasons for this. They have decent markups for the dealer, the above-mentioned privacy and lack of reporting standards, and the double kick of the bullion- and scarcity-appreciation.

You still need to own some junk silver and some gold coins, despite the reporting requirements. The lack of privacy from government prying will not be significant until you actually sell them, and that will be near the peak of any big economic crisis in the future, so it is a relatively minor point. But it is a legitimate issue.

Once you decide what coins you want to buy, be sure to compare prices, just like bullion. They may differ on any given day. You don't necessarily need the very cheapest; close is good enough.

CHAPTER 14

WHAT COULD GO WRONG?

I t's now no secret that I am all-out bullish on gold and silver. I hope that I have made a persuasive case for them, since I feel that you can make a bundle by betting on the metals. But what about the other side? What could go wrong?

Some of the emails I have received express fears that are shared by a lot of people. It has been truly said of the stock market that "it climbs a wall of worry," meaning that along the way to new heights, the bears do at least have an argument. Even if you are positive about the metals, you should at least keep your eye on the possible downside. There *is* a possible downside, and bulls like me had better have an answer to the bearish arguments.

Let's examine some of the scary downside questions.

• **"Howard, might not the government call in all the gold as Roosevelt did in the '30s and take away my gold?"**

While this is possible, is it probable? A look back at the '30s would be instructive. Then we were on a gold standard, and the currency was tied to gold and redeemable in gold. Gold was still considered by everyone to be real wealth, and Roosevelt was trying to head off a recession that at the time was deepening into the Great Depression. At stake was the public's perception of the government's financial stability. Roosevelt ostensibly felt that the best way to achieve this was to have the government own all the gold to strengthen the country's balance sheet. So they made it illegal for citizens to own gold, and we had to surrender our personal metals.

It was a relatively easy chore back then. There weren't that many substantial gold holders then, and they just had to take their gold to the bank.

Now things are very different. Confiscation would be next to impossible to enforce. There are many millions of gold holders, and it would be a political disaster of epic proportions. Uncle Sam doesn't have the personnel or the organization to do it.

In January of 1975, gold was legalized again. There had been a free international marketplace for the metals for a few years prior to that, and the international market price there had risen sharply above our official $35 an ounce.

Now, let's go "back to the future," to the here and now. Gold is now officially just another commodity. Silver in their official opinion is now just another industrial metal with a shrinking stockpile. It would be like seizing copper or zinc. Gold and silver are no longer officially considered to be monetary metals, although the world's central banks are again starting to be buyers for their stockpiles

Today, Uncle Sam is relentlessly campaigning to make gold just another commodity–an investment. In fact, the government is selling gold coins–eagles–made from Fort Knox gold, and they have an aggressive marketing campaign for them. Although they made a bow in the direction of anti-gold when they said you could not put bullion and coins in your IRA, they made an exception for the gold coins they were selling–American eagles!

Gold-mining stocks and mutual funds are now an established part of the financial scene. The mining industry is a big employer, and millions of Americans are holders of the metal. Gold is not yet on the Wall Street buy list, but it is part of the warp and woof of the American financial scene.

Where is the incentive for government to call in the gold? To them, it is no longer money; it no longer backs the currency and is just another commodity they are trying to sell. There is no reason for them to confiscate your gold and destroy an industry. There are a lot of legitimate things to worry about, but confiscation is not one of them.

If you are still concerned about confiscation, buy semi-numismatic coins, as described in Chapter 13.

Homeland Security now has a set of guidelines in case of a sudden collapse of the economy. If that happens, or a general war breaks out, or terrorists pull off a nuclear attack on America, etc., FEMA will have the authority to tell the banks to refuse to let you remove a list of items from your safety deposit box. These include guns, cash, gold and silver. But there is an exemption for semi-numismatic coins, just as there was in

Roosevelt's day. If the coin has a rarity premium greater than 15 percent of the coins market value, it is deemed to be "a collectible," and that's OK.

If you are still nervous about confiscation, don't put your coins in a bank-safe deposit box. Where is up to you. I don't want to know.

• **"But Howard, do you remember when Carter tried to destroy the gold bull market in the'70s by publicly announcing that Uncle Sam would be selling some of the gold in Fort Knox? You yourself raged in *The Ruff Times* about this anti-free market move. Based on the hostile public reaction, they finally backed off, and gold continued to soar. But if gold and silver are going out of sight, what's to prevent them from doing the same thing again?"**

The answer is the same: where is the self interest? Why would they want to do that? What would that gain them? Gold is now not officially "money," just a "commodity," so why interfere with the performance of a commodity? In the case of silver, they couldn't dump any onto the market anyway because they don't have any inventory left to dump. The government silver cupboard is bare!

If you are worried about them dumping gold, buy silver. Would the Feds change their minds if silver soared to $100 an ounce? I don't know for sure, but I doubt it. If they decide to do such a thing, I hope I own some at the time.

• **"But Howard, I have heard there are millions of tons of silver in Mexico and India. What if they should dump their holdings?"**

I am in close touch with those who are going to develop silver mines in Mexico. They are silver bulls, and they are not worried about the Mexican mines. Also, the silver in India (over a million tons) is not in some government or private warehouse. It is in the form of jewelry held by millions of individual Indians as symbols of their wealth. In order for India to "dump" the silver, millions of individuals would have to decide to sell their jewelry to be melted down.

There are two points to be made:

1) The only thing that would cause the Indians to decide to sell would be much higher prices. So where is the problem?

2) Also, as the interest in the metals grows, and more and more investors get more and more worried about monetary inflation, soaring demand and volume will soak up all the new supplies

• **"Howard, what if the alleged low silver inventory figures are wrong? And what if some big mine finds a new Comstock lode of silver? Wouldn't that drive the price down instead of up?"**

The inventory figures come from The Silver Users Association. It is not in their self-interest to tell us that the silver cupboard is nearly bare if they think it isn't so, a fact that they are acutely aware of. To the contrary, in fact, they have even fought the new silver ETF, because they felt that would attract new buyers into the silver market. The ETF would compete with them for the available supplies to meet their industrial requirements and drive up the price. The supply/demand data will eventually drive up the market price, and they wouldn't want that because they have to buy more and more of the stuff for industrial applications, and they want it as cheap as possible. The bullish shortage figures work against that self-interest, so you can bet that they are an unpleasant fact of life for silver users. If there is a bias, it would have to be in favor of *more* silver available, not less.

Even if the shortages are overstated, that's OK too. In the '70s, silver went from $2 to $50 when it was generally believed that there was many times more silver than gold above ground. One indigestible fact of life is that silver production has sagged for 22 or so years, and we are using more silver than we are mining. It is *demand* that will drive silver, not supply.

And what if they find a new Comstock Lode? Let's assume they did. Any such news would be transitory at best. It takes years to bring a new silver discovery into production, perhaps as much as a decade. The supply/demand realities would still be there for years. Also, new silver from even a big strike would be a drop in the bucket as far as meeting demand is concerned. In the meantime, we would still benefit from demand staying ahead of supply for years to come.

CHAPTER 14

Prudent Concern

We can't just dismiss these concerns out of hand. We have to keep our eye on them. Traders will try to take advantage of bearish "facts" and drive down the price. That is why you should not expect the metals to go up every day. All bull markets have their ups and downs. In the '70s it took guts to tough out the retreats (as much as 30 percent), and use them as buying opportunities. Gold and silver will be volatile, but they will remain a "buy-and-hold-and-buy-on-dips" investment for the foreseeable future.

CHAPTER 15

WHEN WILL IT ALL BE OVER? CASHING IN YOUR FORTUNE

What about the signs of the times? I have been asked over and over again, "when will we sell?" I'm reminded of a sign I saw in a restaurant in Oklahoma many years ago, "Lord grant me the gift of patience, and I want it right now."

It will in all likelihood be several years from now. We are very early in this bull market, and gold bull markets usually run for several years. Also the forces that have created this gold and silver bull market are getting bigger, not smaller. A lot will depend on whether monetary inflation continues to rise as it is, or gets completely out of control.

Will we get a sudden rush of brains to the head, and stop demanding benefits from the public treasury that can only be met by creating more cyber-dollars? Will we grow weary of inflation and demand real changes that will stop it in their tracks? Will we keep going into debt like there is no tomorrow? Will we find a new Paul Volcker and a new Ronald Reagan? Will a general war break out?

Will the silver supply/demand situation be solved by big new mines? Will we suddenly find substitute industrial metals and rebuild our silver stockpiles?

Most of these things are completely unpredictable, and only time will tell. That's why I write *The Ruff Times*.

I got a letter from a man who heard me on a talk show in the '70s when gold was about $500. He was convinced and bought some gold coins. Unfortunately, he tried to save a few bucks and didn't subscribe to *The Ruff Times*, so he didn't know when I said to sell his gold. So he hung on to his coins as gold peaked at $850, and then slid back down below $400. He sent me his letter, angrily blaming me for his losses as gold went down and down.

This might seem self serving to you, but I refuse to be accountable to those who run through stop signs, or are driving blind. You can't know when I believe the trend has run its course if you are not hearing from me regularly.

A History Lesson

I have learned a lot from revisiting the history of the '80s, as well as my stubborn mistakes in The Ruff Times, as the metals' bull market slowly died away. The biggest lesson? Only luck gets you out at the exact top. But this time we will be looking through the clarifying looking glass of history, which tells me that it will be different this time than it was in the '80s. It always is. But there are as few enduring lessons from the past.

History tells us that in the 1980s, Paul Volcker (the Fed chairman) and Ronald Reagan were starting to break the back of the monetary inflation that had driven price inflation. Reagan was forcing Congress to slash spending to cut into the government deficits that were behind a lot of the money creation, and Volcker was slowing down the printing presses. Gold and silver were peaking out and beginning what turned out to be a multi-year retreat. Consumer price increases were starting to moderate, so the underpinnings of the gold and silver markets were crumbling, and the underlying monetary inflation was obviously easing.

Also, COMEX in desperation had changed the rules to make silver impossible to rise any more so that they could defeat the Hunt Brothers' attempt to corner the silver market. I knew they had to, because members of the COMEX Board of Governors were all short silver, with futures losses mounting every day as silver soared, and they were insolvent. It was COMEX or the Hunts.

I remember when I appeared at a conference in Fort Worth right after my sell signal, speaking to a club of oil zillionaires. Who should come up and talk to me after my speech but Herbert Hunt, one of the notorious Hunt brothers. He told me he was a *Ruff Times* subscriber, and asked, "Why did you tell everyone to sell their silver?"

I told him that I knew of their battle with COMEX and said, "when the elephants are fighting, we mice head for the underbrush." I also told him that I knew COMEX would change the rules and break the back of the silver market. "You can't fight city hall."

He smiled very condescendingly and said, "We'll win, and silver is going to $100. You'll be sorry for this sell order."

His cocksureness only convinced me that I had done the right thing.

All the signals told me the current was too hard for the metals to swim against. It won't happen just the same way next time, but the peak will send out unmistakable signals.

The result? Just as in 1980, it will end one of the most profitable market episodes in history, only it will probably be much more profitable this time. And it won't be just the insiders who will walk away with the money, but the middle-class amateur investors (*Ruff Times* subscribers?) who will be laughing all the way to the bank.

So peering ahead from early 2006, what will I be looking for this time?

I depend on two basic tools, the charts (technical analysis), and the political environment (fundamental analysis). I only know that it will be different this time. They will either have to get monetary inflation under control, or the sad trends will run their course and end in collapse. We will also get out when we can buy up real assets on the cheap with the proceeds.

The threat of general war will need to have receded, and the currency will need to have recovered. We may have to accommodate a new currency, preferably gold-backed.

Back in 1980, we barely averted an inflationary disaster because of the courage and sound principles of Paul Volcker and Ronald Reagan.

Incidentally, I had an encounter with Paul Volcker that told me he was just the kind of stubborn and arrogant man that would do what it would take to swim against the strong tide of politics and fight monetary inflation while dodging the slings and arrows of outrageous fortune (critics and naysayers).

Meeting Volker

I was in Washington for a Board meeting of RuffPAC, our free-market political-action committee. I called my friend, Senator Paula Hawkins of Florida, and told her I wanted to drop in and say hello.

She said, "I have to go to a reception at the Mexican Embassy in honor of the new Mexican ambassador. My husband is out of town, and I need an escort. Will you go with me?"

"Sure," I said, so we went. There was a huge crowd milling around with drinks in their hands. As I looked around to see if there was anyone I knew, I spotted a very tall man, about six- foot-seven, and saw him hit his head against a low-hanging chandelier, not once but twice.

Paula said, "That's Paul Volcker, the Federal Reserve Chairman. Let me introduce you to him."

As we approached, he saw Paula, and said to her, "Little lady…" (imagine the arrogance of addressing a U.S. Senator that way) "Little lady, when you introduce a banking bill in the Senate, you ought to know a little bit about banking."

Paula, in her best poor-southern-girl voice said, "Paul, I may not be very smart, but I would have only hit that chandelier once." He turned on his heel and disappeared into the crowd. I had my impression of Paul Volcker. He didn't give a damn what anyone thought, and he was going to do what he thought he should. And nothing short of that would save the country from itself.

I guess the answer to our question is: I don't know what the details will be, and I won't know those details until the time is at hand. But I do know that all things being equal, there will have to be a dramatic reversal of the trends that gave us this bull market. Let's just hope that the world has hung together and it is a better day. Let's also hope that we have kept our balance and our principles straight.

How Much Should I Invest?

I am often asked, "How much should I invest in gold and silver and mining stocks?" Unfortunately, there is no one answer. There are too many personal variables in your life. I don't know how old you are, your risk tolerance, how many there are in your family, how much money you have, whether or not you have invested in any of the other things I have recommended, and your debt position, etc. But there are a few principles for you to consider. Assuming that you are persuaded to incorporate some metals into your portfolio, which ones should you choose from among the alternatives? Gold, silver, bullion, coins, stocks, etc?

First Things First

There are some things you should do before you invest in anything for profit. If you have enough money to follow all my advice:

- **Pay off your debts first.** I have outlined a program for painlessly paying off your debts in my book, *Safely Prosperous or Really Rich?*—which you get free when you subscribe to *The Ruff Times*, or you can buy it from Amazon.com for $17.95. Ideally, you should have no consumer debt from credit cards, charge accounts, car loans, etc. Take care of those things first, which are my published priority guidelines. If, after having done that, you have more money each month that is not tied up in interest payments, you can start investing monthly in a gold mutual fund, or some silver coins. You can increase the amount each month as loans are paid off and payment money becomes available for investment.

- **Have some cash on hand.** You need at least $1,000 in greenbacks hidden at home, even if they are being inflated into uselessness. If you are paying on a mortgage (preferably a fixed-rate), you will be able to make your payments with paper, even if the currency goes to hell in a handbasket. The lender will have to accept the payments, even if they become worthless because of inflation. Dollars will still be legal tender.

- **Have a "cash equivalent,"** such as a money-market fund, in a rising interest-rate environment. The amount depends on your personal circumstances.

- **Have an emergency commodity storage program**, just in case of an emergency. I have always recommended you have on hand a six-month supply of non-perishable food and other commodities for each member of the family (diapers, batteries, soap, etc.) at all times. This is part of your survival-insurance program. There is a lot more about this in "Safely Prosperous or Really Rich?"

- **Now, after we have taken care of first things first, we can look at the metals,** starting with junk silver, using the guidelines described in Chapter 3. This is not for investment, but for insurance. After that, we can start investing in bullion or stocks. I like a mixed bag of choices–gold or silver bullion coins, mining stocks, semi-numismatic coins, ETFs and mining mutual funds. I have listed in Chapter 11 a partial menu of stocks and mutual funds to choose from. I update this in *The Ruff Times* every three weeks. I have no hard and fast rules, except that you should be biased in favor of silver stocks.

- **You could diversify with my other industry-group recommendations.** In *The Ruff Times* you will learn about uranium stocks, alternative-energy stocks, commodity-based stocks, (such as copper, zinc, nickel, molybdenum, etc.), oil trusts, etc. and other choices as the times dictate. They should all be winners, and some of them will be big winners.

No-No's

It is time to say goodbye to the stocks that make up a big part of the major stock indices! Even blue chips. The stock market in general will be in the tank, and you should get out of its way. That includes blue chips, utilities, etc. Sure some of them will go up, but most of them won't, and many of them will head south. Even if they do appreciate, mining stocks will do a heck of a lot better.

Other no-no's include any other fixed-rate investments, such as holding fixed-rate mortgages (as opposed to having a fixed-rate mortgage on your home, which is a good idea). When interest rates go up, those things go down, and interest rates will be rising for the foreseeable future. If you are investing in them for income, you will find you are losing more in capital gains than you are making in interest. There is a lot more about investing for income in an inflationary world in Chapter 12.

Thinking short-term should also be a no-no. This book is about a long-term trend; I am not a short-term trader. I prefer to identify a long-term trend and stick with it. Betting on the short-term is hard to do, and I am not much good at it. "Long-term" means investing in rising interest rates, inflation, a falling stock market, and a changing world. Jim Dines once got a big laugh when he said, "a trend in motion will remain in motion until it ends." Funny, but a profound truth for long-term investors. Stay with the trend until you are sure it has ended.

This book does not address your total money position, but a corner of it. It tells you where the best bets are for the future, but they do not exist in a vacuum. The overall picture is an issue for another day in *The Ruff Times*, and I have just touched on it here.

Perhaps the most important criteria for your decision will be based on a gut check—do you feel safer with gold and silver, or paper decorated with ink?

False Alarms

There will be many false sell indications along the way. Some will come out of Wall Street, given their hostility to the metals, and because they are commission-driven and want you to trade in and out.

Prepare yourself for a lot of volatility. In the '70s bull market I saw some dramatic declines of as much as 30 percent and they scared the heck out of me. But hey, I was young then. I even panicked and got out once for a little while. The one big lesson I learned was that I should have bought more on those big dips. So either be patient and wait it out, or add to your holdings. There will be heaven-sent retreats which are opportunities in disguise.

My Parting Shot

I have only known a few people who ever got rich investing, and they did it in the '70s in the metals. You have one of those chances to get rich in the markets that come along once or twice in a lifetime. Take it, and be grateful you live in such a day when you can have a license to print money.

Good luck and God bless.

APPENDIX A

Other Valuable Sources of Information, and Investment Recommendations

ADVISORY NEWSLETTERS

"**The Ruff Times.**" $159 a year for email subscribers, $189 a year for snail-mail subscribers. You can subscribe online. There are some valuable free premiums on the website. P.O. Box 441, Orem, UT 84059; (877) 665-6818, (801) 491-4075; www.rufftimes.com.

"**Richard Russell's Dow Theory Letters**" Written by a wise old pro. An indispensable source of market information. (858) 454-0481; www.dowtheoryletter.com.

"**Casey Research**" Doug Casey is a very savvy and entertaining writer with an encyclopedic knowledge of mines and metals. We have often tangled on values, but never on investments. (800) 528-0559, www.caseyresearch.com.

"**The Aden Forecast,**" by Pamela and Mary Anne Aden. They are also old timers, and their regular newsletter is clear and complete, technical but readable, and always right (they agree with me). They are great gals and great friends. (305) 395-6141; www.adenforecast.com.

"**The Silver Investor Report**" by David Morgan; (509) 464-1651; www.silver-investor.com.

"**Jay Taylor's Gold and Technology Report.**" Jay Taylor is a new friend with a towering reputation. (718) 457-1426; www. miningstocks.com

"**Human Events**" A must-read weekly paper for politically concerned conservatives. (800-787-7557; www.humaneventsonline.com.

"**Gold Mining Stock Report**" by Bob Bishop; (925) 284-1165 www.goldminingstockreport.com

"**The McAlvany Intelligence Advisor**" by Don McAlvany. A good guy and a recommended coin dealer. (800) 525-9556; www.publishers-management.com.

"**The Dines Letter,**" by Jim Dines, The Original Gold (now Uranium Bug). An old friend, and a most-entertaining writer and speaker. Another must read! (800) 845-8259; www.dinesletter.com.

"Resource Opportunities," by Lawrence Roulston. Lawrence is sound and thorough, and he did a recent article in The Ruff Times on Uranium stocks. (877) 773-7677; www.resourceopportunities.com.

"The Gold Stock Report," by Dennis Wheeler. (Late Note: Dennis recently passed away; his publisher, Chip Wood, is an old friend and plans to continue.) 800-728-2288.

"Forecast & Strategies," by Mark Skousen. (800) 211-7661; www.mskousen.com.

"Bull and Bear," Dave Robinson and Val Waters; (800) 336-2855 www.bullandbear.com.

INDISPENSIBLE INFORMATION WEBSITES

www.rufftimes.com
> Both free articles and paid-subscription information.

www.321gold.com.
> Great articles on the subject. I may from time to time have an article there.

www.321energy.com.
> From the same source. Oil stocks and alternative-energy info.

www.kitco.com.
> A major recommended coin and bullion dealer, and a source of up-to-the-minute gold and silver quotes and lots of other info.

www.jsmineset.com.
> From Jim Sinclair, one of the old-timers, and a very successful (and rich) writer since the '70s.

www.lemetropolecafe.com
> From Bill Murphy, a controversial but always-listened to writer.

www.gold-eagle.com.
www.thebullandbear.com.
> Great information on gold, silver and other markets.

www.howestreet.com
www.dickdavis.com.

www.gata.org.
Gold Anti-trust Action Committee
www.goldsheetlinks.com.

PRECIOUS METALS DEALERS

Investment Rarities Inc., www.investmentrarities.com. Friends for 30 years; (800) 328-1860, (952) 853-0700.

International Collectors Associates. www.mcalvany.com. (800) 525-9556

KITCO. My regular source of up-to-the-minute gold and silver quotes. www.kitco.com; (877) 775-4826

Camino Coin, http://caminocompany.com; (800) 348-8001.

GOLD MINING STOCK BROKERS

National Securities – James Raby. My broker. An honest source of info on mining stocks for his clients. Trades Canadian and U.S. stocks. (800) 431-4488.

MINING STOCKS

(The following stocks are not a portfolio, but an a la carte menu for you to choose from. It is the pyramid described in Chapter 11. The asterisk indicates a company with more than 50% of its production or properties in North America.)

MUTUAL FUNDS

ASA LTD (ASA). A closed-end fund, owning mostly South African mining shares. Because of the deteriorating political and social situation there, I don't like it as well as the other choices.

Central Fund of Canada Ltd. (CEF). Listed on the American Exchange. It is a pure bullion fund and maintains a ratio of 50 ounces of silver to one ounce of gold. It is a near perfect proxy for bullion which cannot usually be held in an IRA or other tax-protected plan, like you can with CEF.

American Century Global Gold (BGEIX). An open-end, no-load mutual fund, which probably has the lowest expense ratios.

Tocqueville Gold (TGLDX). An open-end, no-load mutual fund.

US Global Investors (USERX): An open-end, no-load mutual fund.

Fidelity Select Gold (FSAGX). An open-end fund.

ETFS (Exchange-traded Funds)

EFTs are funds that are traded on major exchanges. They invest strictly in gold and silver bullion and can be bought or sold just like any other stock. They are the easiest way to invest in gold and silver bullion. The silver ETF is **iShares Silver Trust** (SLV). The gold ETF is **Streettracks Gold Trust** (GLD).

I favor mining companies with more than 50% of production and/or properties in North America because it will reduce the political risk of expropriation.

Don't ignore the other companies entirely; just make sure your portfolio is balanced towards North America. North American stocks have an asterisk in front of them.

BLUE CHIPS: MAJOR GOLD PRODUCERS
(One-million ounces annually or more)

Barrick (ABX). During the recent correction, Barrick has been able to *sharply reduce their exposure* to the hedges that require them to sell new production at $350 per ounce. After their Homestake acquisition, they are now the biggest gold-mining firm in the world.

*Newmont (NEM), **Gold Fields** (GFI), ***Goldcorp** (GG), **Freeport McMoran** (FCX), ***Kinross** (KGC), and **Anglo Gold** (AU).

SECOND-TIER PRODUCERS
(Annual production between 50-thousand and one-million ounces)

*Agnico Eagle (AEM), Bema (BGO), ***Cambior** (CBJ).

DEVELOPMENT COMPANIES

(Mining companies which have found an ore body and are further defining it by drilling, etc. Some have proven reserves in the ground. They are often shopping for a big partner to finance their development or even to sell out to them.)

*Alamos (AGI.TO), **Arizona Star** (AZS.V), **Bear Creek** (BCM.V), ***Farallon** (FAN.TO), ***Miramar** (MNG).

EXPLORATION COMPANIES

(The bottom of the pyramid. Looking for properties to acquire, explore and develop. May eventually be the most profitable to buy.)

Golden Arrow (GRG.V), ***US Gold** (OB), ***Dejour** (DJE.V), ***Rubicon** (RBY), **Madison** (MMR.V).

PURE SILVER MINES

(These stocks will especially be like a license to print money.)

*Hecla (HL) (a giant), **Pan American Silver** (PAAS), **Silver Wheaton Corp.** (SLW.TO), ***Silver Standard Resources, Inc.** (SSRI), and ***Coeur D'Alene Mines** (NYSE:CDE). There are several others in The Ruff Times.

COMBINATION PLAYS

*Phelps Dodge (PD) a huge copper miner, and is also a big silver producer. ***Northern Dynasty Minerals, Ltd.** (NAK). An Alaskan company with an estimated 18-bullion pounds of copper and 15-20 million ounces of gold.

APPENDIX B
About the Author by the Author

If you are going to listen to my views about gold and silver, you have every right to know what kind of a guy I am, so a little bit of history may be appropriate. I have not always been a gold bug.

There is some fun stuff I thought you might enjoy up front, so please indulge me for a few moments. My life has been so full and unusual that I cannot resist reprinting here something I wrote for fun a few years ago, right after a neighborhood barbecue when we played a game where we had to recount things we had done that we thought nobody else there had done. That fun trip down Memory Lane started my memory running wild. Enjoy!

* * * * *

♦ My 1978 book and my newsletter, *The Ruff Times*, helped start and sustain the great gold and silver Bull Market of the 1970s, and I made several hundred percent for my subscribers in the metals! That was my first financial home run. But that's not all I have done.

♦ I once traded one spool of 8-pound-test monofilament fishing line to the chief of a village in the Amazon jungle in return for two monkey-skull necklaces, a blow gun and darts, a bow and arrows and an Anaconda snake skin. And, after consulting with Kay, I respectfully declined the Chief's offer of a night with one of his four wives in return for a second spool.

♦ I've walked through the dramatic story of the death of Rasputin, the Mad Monk, right on the actual murder scene in a restored palace in Leningrad.

♦ I've interviewed (with Jack Anderson) newly elected President Havel of Czechoslovakia in Prague Palace while he was wearing Nike shoes and a UCLA Bruins sweat shirt. He had been a political prisoner until the Iron Curtain went down.

♦ I've visited the Forbidden City and the Great Wall in China, Machu Pichu, the Imperial Palace in Bangkok, wild-game preserves in

Kenya and South Africa, snorkeled on the Great Barrier Reef and watched great sea turtles lay their eggs and their baby turtles hatch.

♦ Ollie North, my Washington staff, and I, persuaded Ronald Reagan to send Stinger missiles to the Afghan Freedom Fighters, which bogged down the Soviet army in Afghanistan for six years, which led to Soviet bankruptcy, which led to Gorbachev withdrawing Russian financial and military support from Eastern Europe, Cuba and Nicaragua, which led to a break-out of freedom, which led to the crash of the Iron Curtain.

♦ I have sung as a featured artist with the Mormon Tabernacle Choir, the Philadelphia orchestra, the National Symphony, and on the Ed Sullivan Show. I also performed in, conducted or directed hundreds of performances of Gilbert and Sullivan operas and became deeply involved with the Utah Lyric Opera society as a performer, director and General Manager, and was a church choir director at age 16.

♦ I had my own national TV talk show and daily two-minute radio commentary in more than 300 markets.

♦ I was called a liar in an angry speech on the floor of Congress by Congressman Neal of South Carolina, and was denounced by Pravda, Tass, and Soviet-controlled radio Kabul as a "radical reactionary."

♦ I once refused a phone call from an angry President Ronald Reagan. He swore at me, and then sent me an unsolicited, personally autographed portrait as a peace offering.

♦ A ruffled Jimmy Carter succeeded in knocking 50 stations off my radio syndicate by threatening them with trouble at license-renewal time if they didn't cancel my show.

♦ I married a celestial woman, Kay. We've been through thick and thin (I used to be thin) for 49 years, probably because we have one thing in common; we're both in love with the same man!

♦ We have given birth to nine children, adopted four teenagers, and helped raise 18 foster children—and endured the heart-breaking death of one child.

♦ I broke up an orphanage run by American pedophiles in Bangkok, which resulted in jailing them and caused an international incident between ABC, me and the Thai government. I set up my own orphanage in Bangkok to take care of the children.

♦ I was on *Donahue, Good Morning America, The Today Show, Merv Griffin, Dinah Shore, Oprah, Regis and Kathy Lee, Crossfire, PBS Late Night, Nightline, Charlie Rose, McNeil-Lehrer, Wall Street Week,* and hundreds of local radio and TV talk shows, many of them multiple times.

♦ I have had dinner with Chiang Kai-Shek and Madame Chiang, the Secretary to the King of Denmark, and President Synghman Rhee, the Father of modern Korea.

♦ I sang the Star Spangled Banner at the White House numerous times as a soloist for the Air Force Band and Singing Sergeants.

♦ I sold 100,000 copies of an album, *Howard Ruff Sings,* with the Osmond brothers and the BYU Philharmonic and A Cappella Choir as my backup groups.

♦ I caught a piranha in the Amazon and ate it (poetic justice?). It tasted like a bluegill.

♦ I've owned nine airplanes, and have logged 3,500 hours as "pilot in command."

♦ I was forced into bankruptcy in 1968 by a newspaper strike, and then paid off $500,000 (plus interest) in debts from which I had been legally discharged. It took me 12 years.

♦ Evelyn Wood personally taught me to read 3,000 words per minute, and I then developed the marketing and advertising which made her famous.

♦ I cruised the Mediterranean with Art Linkletter.

♦ I took over Madame Tussaud's Wax Works in London one night for a private party for my subscribers, and Kay and I flew to Ireland just to spend a weekend in a castle with Elizabeth Taylor. Unfortunately, she didn't show, so we spent a weekend in a castle in Ireland *without* Elizabeth Taylor.

♦ Whenever I think I've accomplished a lot, I just remind myself that when Mozart was my age—he'd been dead for 37 years.

* * * * *

I was born with a wooden spoon in my mouth. My mother was widowed when I was only six months old. We were poor but I didn't know it, because in the depths of the Great Depression everybody else was poor too. We were actually too poor to afford a father. My mom literally took in sewing to feed me and my eleven-years-older brother Jim. By the time I was nine-years old, I knew what I wanted to be when I grew up: a writer? a financial advisor? A Prophet of Doom? None of the above! I was a really good boy soprano, and I knew I wanted to be a singer on Broadway or at the Met someday.

When I was a pre-adolescent during World War II, we lived in Reno, Nevada and I became a member of the Victory Boys, a group of boy sopranos. We gave patriotic programs all over the state of Nevada. That's when I found what I loved the most in the whole world— applause!!

When I was 13, we moved back to Oakland where my voice changed abruptly from soprano to baritone. So at age 16, I joined a San Francisco musical-theatre company and a year or two later sang in San Francisco's famous opera clubs for $10 a night plus tips. We would sing operatic arias and duets by request from 9:00 p.m. to 2:00 a.m. It was really just a smoke-filled bar, but I was doing what I loved to do.

When I was 18, my voice teacher told me she had arranged for a full-ride scholarship to the Curtis School of Music in Philadelphia. Curtis was considered on a par with Julliard, and could be a very important step on my road to the Met, but when I told my Mom, she threw a big monkey wrench into the works: "But you are supposed to go on a mission!" As a practicing Mormon family, it was expected that young men would volunteer to leave home for two years and teach the gospel to potential converts, and I didn't want to go because I knew that my Curtis scholarship would be toast.

After a period of intense spiritual inquiry, I finally made the hard decision that unbeknownst to me would change the whole direction of my personal and professional life. I decided that if I served the Lord, He would take care of me, so with blind faith, I launched out into the dark and decided on the mission. They sent me to the heathens—Washington D.C.—and not only did it jump-start my lifelong interest in government, economics and politics, but it was there that I first heard the Air Force Band and Singing Sergeants in a Sunday night concert on the Capitol steps, which would change my life forever. I was also befriended by the two senators from Utah, Arthur Watkins and Wallace Bennett (the father of Utah's present senator), and J. Willard Marriott Senior of hotel fame. We had had long discussions about life, business and the issues of the day and I began forming my economic, business and political opinions. I attended the Missionary School of Hard Knocks—on thousands of doors— and learned one of the great lessons of life that every salesman and marketer must learn—how to live with continuous rejection and failure and keep bouncing back day after day. It was a tough but immensely satisfying and character-building experience, and I regretted it coming to an end.

After my mission, I went to BYU to continue my musical education. When I ran out of money after my junior year, I went back to San Francisco where my mother now lived, to make some money so I could go back to school, singing in the opera clubs by night and selling Chryslers by day. Then, unexpectedly, I was reclassified 1-A in the draft and ordered to report for induction into the army. I remembered the Air Force Singing Sergeants, called the Pentagon to get their phone number in Washington D.C., and was given the number of Col. George S. Howard, Chief of Bands and Music for the Air Force. I called him. He told me he had an opening coming up for a new baritone soloist, but wouldn't be in California for six months, so I told him, "I'll audition in Washington next Wednesday."

I borrowed $150 from my big brother, flew to Washington, auditioned, got the job (with a letter to prove it!), and enlisted in the Air Force. After only three weeks of basic training, I was ordered to report to Washington to go with the Air Force Symphony on a tour of Iceland and Scandinavia as soloist and announcer. I called the lovely Kay Felt in San Francisco and rather arrogantly informed her we would be married in Salt Lake City on the way to Washington the following Monday.

Fortunately, she couldn't think of any good reason why not, so we were married on schedule. Kay Felt became Kay Felt Ruff (when she realized what her name would be, it almost killed the marriage). She has been the spiritual and nurturing center of my life and family, and our numerous kids (thirteen living, including five adopted as teenagers) and grandkids (65 at last count). All adore her—and so do I. I may be the head of my traditional family, but she is the heart.

I traveled all over the world with the band, meeting and in some cases having dinner with such historical figures as Chiang Kai Shek,

Synghman Rhee (the founder of modern South Korea), and assorted prime ministers and royalty on three continents and twenty countries We also toured in 48 states. I was having an amazing educational experience, while Kay was at home having babies.

But I wasn't really an absentee father. Being a Singing Sergeant was a government job, so when we weren't on tour (we were only gone about 15 weeks out of the year), we only had to report for two hours a day for rehearsals, so I got a job with a stock broker, continuing my economic and financial education, and spent a lot of time at home, helping Kay with the kids and learning to love fatherhood.

When my four-year hitch was up, we moved to Denver to work for my broker/employer, stumbled across Evelyn Wood Reading Dynamics, bought the Denver franchise, then the Bay Area franchise, and launched my business career, teaching the world to read faster and more efficiently. I learned I had valuable gifts as a marketer, writer and public speaker, but I was also laying the foundation for my first big Learning Experience—a business failure!

We'd had eight glorious years, with more than 10,000 students in the San Francisco Bay area, and I wrote the ads and designed the marketing for all the nationwide franchises. I became the protégé of Evelyn Wood, who taught me how to read over 3,000 words-per-minute, a life-changing skill that has served me well ever since. We taught law students at the University of California and Stanford, high school and junior-high students and businessmen, how to read more rapidly and efficiently and both enjoy and absorb more from their reading. As the money was rolling it, we spent it. We gave money to the Oakland Symphony, and I bought Kay a $1,000 designer dress so that when we had our picture on the society page at post-concert receptions, she would look great. In the meantime, our family was continuing to grow, and Kay bore more much-loved and much-wanted children.

However, I was making the biggest mistake of my life to that date, (although bigger mistakes would come later). Because I thought the gravy train would last forever, we didn't bother to accumulate any savings or cash reserves. We had good credit and used it. We spent our money as if there was no tomorrow, or, to be more accurate, I did.

Kay expressed her concerns which I discounted because I thought I knew better.

Then disaster struck. I had planned an eight-page advertising supplement to go into all of the Bay Area newspapers one Sunday. On Friday night a wild-cat strike hit all the Bay Area papers, and the Sunday paper was never published. I had spent $25,000 printing that supplement, which at the time seemed like all the money in the world, and we couldn't just keep them and use them at a later time because they were all geared toward specific demonstration meetings on specific dates at specific places all over the Bay Area.

I was in deep trouble. I didn't have any cash reserves, accounts payable began to pile up, we were up to our ears in hock and personal debt, and I was in arrears with my royalties. Finally the parent company, seeing an opportunity to grab off the business and resell it to someone else, abruptly cancelled my franchise and notified the sheriff. My doors were locked and I was out of business. I went to work rich and came home broke. It ruined my whole day.

This forced me into bankruptcy, but Kay and I, prompted by some ethical counseling by local church leaders, decided that even though we had filed bankruptcy, legally discharging half-a-million dollars in debt, we would not be right with our creditors and the Lord if we didn't someday pay it off. So I made perhaps the most important decision of my life—I would eventually pay off those debts. This meant I couldn't just get a J.O.B.; I had to become rich—again. That all happened in October 1968, and we had already been hit by a tragedy the previous June when our toddler, Ivan, was drowned in our swimming pool. This was a devastating year, but I now know that sometimes the healing and correcting spirit of God can only enter us through our gaping wounds. This spiritual process had begun at Ivan's death when we had to decide what we really believed. We were ready to make the spiritual, financial and emotional commitment to pay off half a million dollars in debt. It took us twelve years to pay for that dead horse, but we did it! This lesson has had a profound impact on this book, especially the second half, as it illustrates two of its most important principles, including the principle that *the first step in getting rich is simply to decide to do it,* which is what I did.

In the meantime, we had taken in a teenaged foster son in the neighborhood who had become estranged from his family. The word got around, so over the following years we took in more than 18 of them, mostly teenagers, for varying lengths of time. We eventually adopted five.

I began my business comeback as a distributor in the multi-level sales organization for a major manufacturer of food supplements, The Neo Life Company, which is still in existence today and is one of the honorable survivors of the multi-level-marketing business. I quickly became its largest distributor and won all of the company awards for performance. This began a lifelong obsession with keeping up with the research and development of nutritional supplements.

About this time, I began to worry about what I saw as a coming train wreck for the economy.

When I was in an airport, I saw a book whose title intrigued me, "How to Prepare for the Coming Crash" by Robert Preston. Thinking it was a way to stay safe if the airplane went down, I bought it to read on the plane, but that wasn't the crash it was talking about. Preston advocated investing in silver and gold as a hedge against an inflation-induced economic crash. For the first time my stock-market-oriented brain began to turn in that direction. I began to study the fundamentals of Austrian economics and the inflation that would lead to economic troubles and a resurgence of gold. I began to worry about what I believed the government was doing to the economy with its inflationary policies.

I also became convinced that there was a real possibility of a deep recession that could turn into a depression, characterized by high inflation and unemployment. I became a vocal advocate of emergency food-storage as a kind of family-insurance program. After all, we had once lived on our stored food when the bottom had dropped out of our financial lives in 1968. This traditional Mormon practice grew not so much out of its theology as it did out of its 19th century pioneer self-sufficiency culture. It was not an apocalyptic practice, but a very practical one, designed for just the kind of circumstances we had to face. This very prudent, riskless piece of financial advice planted the roots of what would someday be the cause of my near-universal bad press.

I wrote my first book, a very bad self-published book called "Famine and Survival in America," not realizing how powerful words could be. Rather than a carefully reasoned discussion of why you ought to have a food-storage program as a conservative, prudent precaution against hard times for your family, it sounded more like a scream in the night. But to my amazement, as I began to do radio and TV shows to promote this self-published book, it caught on as people were scared of what was happening in the world around them as inflation soared.

In the book I promised to send a monthly update on the markets to book buyers, so I soon was sending out 5,000 monthly updates and going broke doing it. I sold off my supplement distributorship to finance a for-pay newsletter, which I called *The Ruff Times* to a chorus of sardonic jeers. My guts told me that name was right for our times. I launched *The Ruff Times* newsletter in June 1975, forecasting rising inflation, a falling stock market and rising gold and silver prices, and was I ever right! At the time, gold was only $120 an ounce and silver was under $2. They had not yet begun the spectacular bull market that would take them to $850 and $50 respectively.

As the precious metals and *The Ruff Times* took off, I decided I needed to write a manual for new subscribers because you couldn't reinvent the wheel every time you went to press. With no intention of publishing it as anything but a manual for new subscribers, I wrote *How to Prosper During the Coming Bad Years*. A member of my board of directors knew many New York publishers, so he persuaded me to go there to meet several of them. Four of them wanted to publish the book. I chose Times Books, a division of the *New York Times* of all things. Tom Lipscomb, the president, was a brilliant publisher and marketer who believed passionately in me and the book and shared my philosophy. He and I made publishing history together—three million copies!

By this time I had a syndicated TV talk show on 350 stations called *Ruffhou$e*, interviewing a lot of interesting guests. I got a call from a radio syndicator who had been distributing the Ronald Reagan daily radio commentary. When Reagan decided to run for President, he gave up his radio show, so they asked me to fill that slot, as I was getting a lot of notoriety as the book hit the top of the New York Times best-seller list and my TV show was gathering millions of viewers.

So I created a two-minute daily radio commentary, which eventually was on some 300 stations. *The Ruff Times* was on its way to the stratosphere—or so I thought!

As a public service to benefit from my high profile and high levels of trust from my like-minded subscribers, I founded RuffPAC, a political action committee, and Free The Eagle, a registered lobby in Washington D.C. I began to fight for free-market issues and free-market-oriented candidates for public office. We were successful in some pretty important things, such as persuading President Reagan to get stinger missiles to the Afghan rebels. This forced the Soviets to fly so high they wouldn't devastate the villages that were harboring the Mujahadin. It stalemated the war. When the body bags kept going home and the Soviet Union was on the verge of bankruptcy trying to support their functional equivalent of our Vietnam, eventually Gorbachev withdrew from Afghanistan, pulled back the Soviet Army from their Iron Curtain satellites, stopped their financial support of Cuba, the Sandinistas in Nicaragua, and communist insurgent groups in Africa, and the Iron Curtain began to crumble. I honestly believe we had something to do with starting that whole process.

In any event, *The Ruff Times* had become a publishing phenomenon. *How to Prosper During the Coming Bad Years* was #1 or #2 on the hard-cover best-seller list for months, and when the paperback came out a year later, it not only stayed on or near the top of the hard-cover list, but was also #1 on the paperback list. It stayed high on both lists for two years.

Early on, the Prophet (sometimes spelled "Profit" by the media) of Doom title began to plague me. It seems that the hardcore "survivalists" were getting a lot of media attention. These extremists shared some of my economic views (gold, silver, stored food, etc.), but they believed that society would collapse completely, so they were building impregnable retreats in the mountains and buying lots of guns and storing food and hunkering down, waiting for the end. I had a chapter in *How to Prosper During the Coming Bad Years* about the advisability of a food-storage program as a riskless, prudent hedge against personal or public financial difficulties, and a lot of information on how to invest in gold and silver. There it was; guilt by association!

The simple-minded media saw me as a hook for critical stories about hardcore survivalists, and the Prophet of Doom title was forever attached to me, despite my protests. Heck, the "How to Prosper," in the title, which is not exactly an end-of-the-world idea, should have been a clue to them that they were wrong, but to no avail.

I continued to publish *The Ruff Times*, but to save money, I then decided to take it to the Internet.

My Biggest Professional Flop?

The Y2K crisis! I believed that this was a deadly serious threat and could have devastating effects on the economy. I said so in my letter, and even wrote a book on the subject. I was dead right about the seriousness of the problem, but for the only time in my life, I underestimated the willingness and the ability of government and industry to solve the problem in time to beat the deadline of January 1, 2000. Miraculously, they did fix it in time, due to the efforts of Senator Bob Bennett of Utah and others. On New Year's Day, 2000, when the dire consequences failed to materialize, I had egg all over my face, and that book became a big publishing flop. It wasn't that I had not analyzed the problem properly; it was that I didn't believe that they would have the will and the smarts to fix it in time. I was wrong, big time!

My Biggest Triumphs?

But it's not all bad. There were many triumphs, but two stand out:

Way back in 1975 when I started publishing *The Ruff Times*, I fore-saw the coming inflation that plagued us for the next seven years, and analyzed, correctly, that it would cause a big boom in gold and silver and recommended gold when it was only $103 an ounce and silver when it was under $2. Gold subsequently went to $850 and silver to $50 for a few days in 1980. For 22 years, gold went sideways or down.

I turned bullish on the stock market in 1983, mostly because of Ronald Reagan, and stayed bullish for several years. We did very well for my subscribers, but I started telling people to get out of the stock market about six months before it peaked in March 2000 and called the market an "unsustainable mania and a bubble." This was right on the money, as March 2000 was the peak of the greatest bull market in history, and the beginning of the greatest bear market in history. I've been on the right side of that market ever since, keeping people out of it, and instead recommending thirty-year T-bonds and ten-year T-notes, where we had big profits in 2000-2003, and saved them untold millions of dollars.

In 1983 I was at the top of my popularity. My book was number one on the bestseller lists in both hardcover and paperback and had become the biggest financial bestseller of all time. My syndicated TV show, *RuffhouSe*, was showing in 300 markets, and my two-minute daily radio commentary was on 350 stations. My newsletter, *The Ruff Times*, had more than 175,000 subscribers, and I thought I was a marketing genius, as all the direct-mail pieces I wrote worked. My Washington lobby, Free the Eagle, and RuffPAC, my Political Action Committee, were real powers in Washington. I had access to President Reagan and any Senator and Congressman I wanted to talk to. I was famous, I was rich, and the world was my oyster. But just like the high-tech investors in March, 2000 who thought they were great stock-pickers, it would in retrospect be the high-water mark of my professional and business life. It would be all downhill business-wise from there. Little did I realize that I wasn't the marketing genius I thought I was. I was just a very lucky guy with the right message at the right time, and if conditions changed much, I wouldn't be so smart. Conditions changed!

Ironically, even though I had campaigned vigorously for him and had warm personal relations with him, the election of Ronald Reagan was the beginning of a long, downhill slide for me. I had made my mark in the world by telling people how to prosper during the scary Jimmy Carter-induced inflation of the '70s. Ronald Reagan was my friend, and Jimmy Carter was my foil. Ronald Reagan and Paul Volcker's successful assault on the runaway inflation and interest rates of the late '70s made people less convinced we were facing some "Coming Bad Years," and properly so. My old message was less compelling. As I changed with the times and became properly bullish on America, the new message was less interesting than the old one, and media publicity was harder to come by.

During that years-long downhill slide I made a series of stupid mistakes that taught me most of what I know today. I had learned how to make a fortune, and had done it twice, once in good times and once in bad times. Then I had learned how to *lose* a fortune, and had done that twice—also in good times and bad.

In retrospect, as I became a celebrity, my financial success and notoriety infected me with a bad case of *hubris*—the Greek word for the arrogant pride of the gods. I unconsciously believed that I was so smart I could violate my own published rules with impunity and avoid the problems that would trip up lesser mortals, and my success wasn't teaching me a thing. Too often my operative principle was "do as I say, not as I do." Unfortunately, I was wrong—*really* wrong—which has cost me millions. Much of what I thought I knew that eventually turned out to be wrong came out of my successes.

One reason I felt driven to write this sometimes-embarrassing treatise is that I don't want my posterity to repeat all the foolish mistakes I will tell you about; my successes are nowhere near as instructive and helpful. If I can't pass on what I learned about the things that no longer work—or didn't work in the first place—some of my most valuable experiences would be wasted, and making the mistakes I made will prevent them from becoming Safely Prosperous or Really Rich if they repeat them. I also want the cathartic benefit of publicly facing reality about myself and cramming a little humility down my unwilling throat. It will be too late when I am trying to explain my arrogant pride to God.

Old Fogy Wisdom

This book could only be written by someone of my ripe years (sometimes I wish I were 74 again). I've been observing the world of money through three serious recessions, three major bull and bear markets, including the late, lamented dot-com bubble of 1996-2000, the insane inflation of the 70's, a real-estate boom and bust, a historic gold bull market and subsequent collapse, 14 children (five were adopted—we couldn't find homes for the other nine), 18 foster children, 65 grandchildren and 3 great grandchildren. I've made and lost two fortunes by making some stupid pride-driven mistakes, been written off by Wall Street as a fringe character at times, but for a few glory years, I couldn't walk down any sidewalk in the Wall Street financial district without being recognized. For the last decade, I've been laying low, laboring away in relative obscurity just publishing my newsletter on the Internet, and waiting for gold's inevitable comeback. And my patience has finally been rewarded; hence this book.

In short, in a financial world that has been dominated by 20- and 30-something kids who weren't even stockbrokers during the last bear market in 1987, I'm one of a small clique of *real adults*–newsletter writers, financial publishers, analysts and advisors–who are old enough to have been around since the '60s and '70s, and through the gold and silver bull market of the '70s.

Now I'm back, and so are the metals. Remember, they are a middle-class license to print money

A Real Adult: I've Been There

I have been publishing The Ruff Times through 31 years of Bull and Bear markets in the precious metals, unlike most of the hot financial advisors and brokers during the late, lamented Bull Market, who are so young they weren't even born yet. They were the Invincible Optimists at the peak of the last Bull Market on Wall Street in the spring of 2000, when I was yelling at them to get out of the stock market. I think I am one of a handful of real adults in the Wall Street kindergarten with a long-range view of the world of money, and an encyclopedic view of gold and silver.

It this book hasn't convinced you of this, then I'm sorry. I tried.

Sign up for The Ruff Times and/or the Ruff Free eLetter

You may register for either or both at www.rufftimes.com.

The Ruff Times is published every three weeks, and contains comprehensive and detailed updates on the Investment Menu for $159 as news dictates, as well as many other articles of interest to middle-class investors. (Deduct ten dollars if you already have a copy of this book, unless you want another one as a free premium for a friend). There are several samples on the website

The Ruff brief eLetter is weekly, typical Ruff-stuff, and deals with a broad variety of issues, including Precious Metals, Politics, Social Issues that may affect your pocket book, Ruffonomics 101, Investing for Income, or whatever interests me that week. Simply post your email address at www.rufftimes.com.

INDEX